TORNADO VALLEY:

Huntsville's Havoc

SHELLY VAN METER MILLER

Editor: Diana Miller
Cover Design by R.E. Miller

ISBN: 1481866680
ISBN-13: 978-1481866682

DEDICATION

This book was written to honor those courageous people in the State of Alabama and all over the country who have suffered immeasurable loss due to violent tornadoes and continue to live their lives serving others who have experienced the same.

ACKNOWLEDGMENTS

Thank you to my husband for supporting me and cheering me on. Thank you to my children for not expecting dinner on the table during the last several months while I was writing. Thank you to Sharon, Laura, Laurel, Brad, Pastor David (for Sonny), and Cindy (for Shannon), for agreeing to be named as the real people they are, while allowing the author to fictionalize their conversations for the purpose of telling their true stories.

CONTENTS

Shelly Van Meter Miller

1
APRIL'S MAYHEM – APRIL 27, 2011

Shelly – Madison, AL 6:30 a.m.

Beep, beep, beep--The chirping alarm announced the time. Still lying in bed, I heard the whirring ceiling fan whose cool draft felt good across my face on this unseasonably warm morning. I waited for it to happen. Like clockwork, the cat catapulted onto our bed, demanding a feast for breakfast. She jingled her collar bell with the flick of a paw as if it were a dinner bell to signal that breakfast was expected. Kitty leapfrogged to my husband's side of the bed, knowing who the early morning pushover was. We both pulled the covers over our heads and fussed at Kitty for patience. She left in a huff, but not before she sharpened her claws on our mattress, just for spite. This ritual began five years ago when we rescued our stray cat from the sewer.

I heard the shower spraying and dozed off again. Another round of alarm beeps jolted me awake. My eyes riveted to the clock face, but instead I saw the cat's face staring at me with her glow-in-the-dark eyes, as if the noisy intrusion was my fault. Remembering that my husband was in the shower, I performed a series of rolls, slammed my fist on the Sony clock that's older than the sun, and silenced the alarm, but not the cat's whining.

"Shush!" I commanded. I tried to concentrate on what came next. It was Wednesday on a warm April day. I wondered what I could drum up for the girls' school lunches. My youngest teen had decided that she was conveniently allergic to peanuts, so no more peanut butter and jelly sandwiches for her. We all questioned her new food allergy. Everyone else her age had a food allergy- no eggs, no gluten, lactose intolerant, or whatever was the fashionable allergy of the week. It could've been worse. Heaven forbid any family member would develop a chocolate allergy. That was unacceptable.

Once I was reprimanded at my daughter's birthday party for serving nuts. One of her friends was allergic to them so I purposely served fruit instead. When I named off each food item, one by one, the guest's mother stopped me in mid-sentence and triumphantly pointed out that a mango was a tree nut. All this time I thought a mango was a fruit. Apparently sometimes it was a nut, and sometimes it was not. Now the "What's for lunch?" question took an energy toll every morning. It would be another salami day ahead, with a Flintstone vitamin for breakfast.

Ww-rr-rr-ee! Another alarm echoed. The cat meowed in protest. "I didn't do it, Kitty," I snapped as the annoying siren penetrated the air. The TV remote was missing in action, so I turned the television on the old fashioned way by finally getting out of bed. I turned to a weather channel as the siren drew my girls out of their own beds and planted them in front of my bedroom television set. Unbelievably, the radar indicated rotation and evidently it was not too early in the morning for a tornado. Forecasters warned that the day might go like this, but the TOR:CON scale didn't mean anything to us on the 27th of April. It would by the end of the day.

"Get Dad out of the shower," I ordered the girls.

"You do it, Mom!" they shouted over the sirens as they tramped down the stairs to the interior bathroom for shelter. Instead of mapping out our disaster plan, I spent precious time luring the cat into the bathroom using a can of Fancy Feast as bait. Seven in the morning was way too early to be prepared for anything. All five family members, six counting the cat, rubbed the sleep out of our eyes while backed into a corner. The girls had smiles plastered across their faces, like cats with canary feathers hanging from their mouths. "What's so funny?" I asked.

"Does this mean that school is cancelled?" they hoped. I sort of hoped so too and wouldn't bother with the salami sandwiches. We endured the gyration of the nervous sirens while Kitty slurped down her breakfast and our stomachs growled. Part of me welcomed the warning sirens as a chance to slow down the week.

Sharon-Harvest, AL 11:45 a.m.

Sharon drifted outside after hand washing the dishes. There was not much else to do after the morning storm passed, taking the neighborhood's electrical power with it. Now the skies were clear and the day was shaping up to be a gorgeous one, sunny and mild. She walked leisurely around the front porch to survey her newly planted flower bed. She purposely waited until Alabama's last frost date of April 15th to plant her marigolds and colorful annuals. Judging by the looks of the blooms, April showers really did bring May flowers. The smell of fresh mulch lingered when she brushed past.

The early morning storm stirred things up around the yard. Miscellaneous twigs were strewn underneath Jamie's tree, the large maple tree that was planted when her son Jamie was born in 1984. Jamie was now twenty-something and his mature tree shed helicopter seeds all over the yard. Sharon resumed her ritual of picking up sticks and tried to keep up with the seeds propelling from the maple. The neighbor's dog stretched his chain to its full length to bark incessantly at her. The dog never barked while tied up. "Calm down," Sharon commanded. "Do you know something that I don't?" No one else was around but the dog was clearly agitated.

Just then, Sharon's cell phone rang. Her son called to tell her that the weather was supposed to 'get ugly.' "Oh, they always say that," Sharon said. The son worried for his momma since the power was out and she couldn't hear sirens where she lived. He asked if she still had her weather radio. "Yes, but I shut it off because it was so annoying." Sharon complained. She finished her phone conversation with her son and then said a quick prayer while leaning down to gather more maple twigs. "Lord, if I need to go, please make it obvious."

Laura-East Limestone, AL 3:05 p.m.

It was coming. She knew this would happen. It was her dream come true—her bad dream. All week, Laura dreamt of water oozing under the door and the basement of her home flooding. Maybe the dreams stemmed from her second reading of the book, *F5* by Mark Levine. Why she kept turning page after page of the true tornado thriller, she didn't know. But now here she was, lying in wait for a possible common fate.

Laura hadn't been in her new home long enough to get attached to it. She was wary of moving to Alabama in the first place—not because she was a Yankee from Iowa, but because of her past memories of the state. She was only eight years old when she visited her grandma in Guinn, Alabama. She barely remembered what her grandma's house looked like before the 1974 F5 tornado destroyed it. Her memories were those of her grandma's house after the destruction. Everyone said that the small town of Guinn was wiped off the map. Miraculously, her grandma was one of the few townspeople who survived. Laura was haunted by the aftermath still vivid in her memory, although an F5 didn't leave much for the eye to see. An eight year old was frightened by the prospect that an entire town could vanish. It was just as scary to an eighty year old.

That was the reason Laura's family was safe in their underground bunker during April, thirty-seven years later. Laura would move to Alabama on the one condition that they find a home with a basement shelter for such storms. Realtors tried to convince her that basements were not common in the state. Basements were more of a northern thing. Nevertheless, Laura insisted on it and found the perfect home in East Limestone County. The new construction was surrounded by hardwood trees, had acreage for her show dogs to enjoy, and as if a prayer had been answered, it had a finished basement. On April 27, 2011, Laura and her family, along with her show dogs, were hunkered down in that basement, waiting for the inevitable storm that the sirens so earnestly warned about.

The storm was definitely coming. It sounded like a train derailed on the floor above them. The kids held their ears tightly while screaming. Laura texted her loved ones up North: We're in a '#@*!ing' tornado! Her mom in Iowa received the text but was confused. She texted Laura back: What's a 'duckling' tornado? Laura's smart phone was so smart that it converted the bad words into sterile words. Laura texted again: I think we lost the '#@*!ing' house! Her mother still tried to understand: Oh no, what was in the 'filing' house?

Laura gave up texting and held her children and her ears too. "It hurts!" they shrieked. It did hurt. Holding their ears did not relieve the pressure. Their heads felt like they were ready to explode. The basement door protested as well, rattling uncontrollably. Laura saw water oozing under the threshold. Abruptly the door stopped shaking. The air pressure normalized and their ear pressure subsided.

Laura felt that the worst was over. She checked for blood dripping from their ears, but there was none. It was now time to check the rest of the 'filing' house.

Sharon-Harvest 3:10 p.m.

"Get in the truck now!" It was Sharon's husband, not the Lord, who ordered her to leave. Or maybe, it was the Lord. Sharon and her husband jumped in the truck together and wheeled out of the driveway. They turned to go to Sharon's mother's house which had a basement, but they encountered a tornado on the same road! They spun the truck 180 degrees to find an alternate route. Wall Triana Highway was deemed inaccessible with a funnel in one of the lanes.

Sharon watched the tornado follow them as her husband dialed a number on his cell phone. When their neighbor answered the call, Sharon heard her husband shout into the phone, "Take cover now. We see it coming!" They continued to race away from the tornado while they kept their neighbor on the phone. In the background, they heard their neighbor cajoling his unruly dog into the basement with him. Then there was static—the kind that hurts the caller's ear as he yanked the phone away impulsively. "Talk to me!" her husband hollered into the phone. They heard the neighbor scream, but he couldn't hear them.

"My dog, my dog!" the neighbor wailed. "He didn't make it down. He was sucked out the back door!" More static. Finally the neighbor stopped hollering long enough to realize that he still held the phone. He kept mumbling, "It's so dark. It's just so dark."

"Can you see anything?" Sharon's husband asked.

"All I see are trees." One of those was Jamie's tree, but the neighbor didn't know it.

"Can you see my house?" Sharon's husband asked expectantly.

"No, but I see your car."

"That's not good. My car was in the garage."

Shelly-Madison 4:40 p.m.

"Let's roll!" my husband ordered. All day we had taken shelter in our cozy half-bath located on the first floor of our home. I retrieved the children from school before the Superintendent gave parental permission because I intended to have my children with me on such a treacherous weather day. It was a mistake to send children to school with the predictions so dire. A TOR:CON 10 was the highest tornado rating ever issued. The entire state of Alabama would find out what this title meant by the afternoon. It was obvious that our downstairs bathroom would not suffice for the day. We needed to move to lower ground. The answer to our dilemma was our church basement located several miles away, and luckily we had a key to the basement door.

Having the key was a result of too many calls we made to our pastor, disturbing his nighttime sleep during tornado warnings, pleading for him to open the church basement for our family to take shelter. On one occasion, he took the church key off its ring and said, "Just keep it." My husband now stood impatiently in the doorway of our house with keys in hand.

I stood over the cat carrier trying to coax our fat cat inside with some treats like I had done so many times before. My husband jingled the church keys again, then swept past me and grabbed the cat in one swoop. He turned the carrier on its end and shoved the cat's end into the carrier and slammed the caged door. My husband was normally serious about the weather, but this was the most nervous I had ever seen him. Even the cat obeyed him—now that was something.

We drove to the tune of tornado warning sirens all around us. Other cars on the road flashed their hazard lights. Ours joined with the blinking as we rolled through at least two red lights. When passing the Bob Jones High School, I startled my family by exclaiming, "Look at that wall cloud!" There was no mistaking the type of cloud it was. People always said that you would know a wall cloud if you saw one. They were right. The wall of cloud harbored something sinister within. My eyes were glued to it as if expecting a water moccasin snake to drop out of the sky and writhe towards our car, twisting its funnel-shaped body to shed its skin. The clouds moved so quickly and we felt more anxious to get to the church basement while watching the wall cloud which was now in the rear-view mirror.

We continued to speed towards the church and made it underground right before the power surged in a last-ditch effort to maintain electricity. As it failed, only the Exit signs lit the dark basement. We circled folding chairs around a transistor radio and listened intently to the local weather. One of the meteorologists went off the air, obviously shaken when she described the tornado that was terrorizing the town of Eva, AL where her family lived. Instead of thinking her behavior unprofessional, I felt as if the meteorologist was one of us. It made the threat more real to us, knowing that real people were in harm's way. If anything, her emotional lapse caused listeners to heed the warning, possibly saving more lives. The new announcer declared that a funnel was spotted on the corner of Wall Triana Highway and Highway 72. He described our neighborhood! Thank goodness we abandoned our home. Nevertheless, we worried about our empty house.

After receiving a break in the weather, our family followed the Exit signs up the basement stairs and out into the open. The sky was clear as if it was another peaceful day and nothing had happened. We surveyed the church grounds. The iris flower bed next to the church bench was in full bloom. The flowers stood tall on their long stems. There was nothing sweeter than the smell of a fresh iris in spring bloom and reminded me of my Memaw's garden. My daughter commented, "Look, Mom, the flowers still look pretty. That must mean that everything's okay, right?" It would seem so. A light breeze blew, but instead of the expected fresh iris scent, the wind carried a fresh Pine-Sol scent. It reminded me of the ammonia-clean smell after cleaning the bathroom. All was strangely quiet, too quiet. And it was surprisingly calm, dead calm.

Laurel (Near Laura) - East Limestone 4:55 p.m.

"Don't leave this room," Laurel instructed.

"Mom, please don't go!" her children begged.

"We have to check on Grandmommy and Papa," Laurel's voice cracked and she heard the fear in it. She feared both the known and the unknown. She knew that a tornado just passed over her home although the twister was shrouded in rain. She saw transformer sparks as the tornado bowled over the neighborhood across from her, leaving only a couple of trees standing like a pair of missed bowling pins. Then she saw the telltale debris swirling—debris from her property. Her parents lived in that neighborhood too!

She ran for cover with her family into the concrete safe room next to their master bedroom. The safe room saved their lives. But the children cried for their horse, Sammy. Laurel didn't have time to secure the horse in the barn. He was off in the field with the swirling debris. And what of her parents—where were they? A lush forest separated Laurel's long driveway from their subdivision. At least it used to. The last thing Laurel had seen coming up the drive was the tornado.

She and her husband hated to leave the children behind, but the kids were safer where they were. Laurel had to get to her parents. Oh why, oh why didn't her parents listen? No telling how many times her parents lamented the same question about her when she was young. At some point, the tide turns and parents were supposed to listen to their children. Her parents didn't listen when Laurel told them to come to her house and take shelter in her safe room. No amount of pleading could deter Laurel's mother from fixing dinner. The preparations were already behind schedule when they lost power that morning. Her mother was from the generation that always had dinner on the table, come hail or high water.

Laurel's thinking was muddied as she stepped out of her shelter. Confusion met her at the door with muddy floors and total disarray. Her house was in shambles and the carpets sloshed as she trudged through the hallway in her hiking boots. Her husband leaned against the stairwell and fell through the drywall. It was as if the house had melted, leaving the safe room island floating in a giant puddle. She couldn't mourn her house yet. She had to know that her parents were safe.

She and her husband waded through the rest of the house. They blinked continuously, trying to see through the pouring rain. Goggles were needed. Once they were able to see, they couldn't believe their eyes. Laurel looked towards the barn first. It lay crushed under a tree. She panicked even though she knew Sammy wasn't inside. He was nowhere in sight.

Nothing seemed normal, not even the forest she expected to see across the street. Those beautiful trees that used to line her driveway were stacked stories high, blocking the view of the dark sky. Her husband's face indicated that he was yelling to her, but Laurel couldn't hear him with the slanted rain pelting the horse helmet that she still wore for storm protection. Realizing that communicating with her was useless in the driving rain, her husband pointed toward the drainage ditch. They would have to tread through the mire to reach her parents' neighborhood. They took turns pulling each other through the muck. Finally out of the mud pit, Laurel glanced down and noticed that her husband was shoeless. Her boots stayed on her feet, but they felt like sacks of flour strapped to her ankles, weighted down with clotted clay, our wet Alabama soil. They each spotted a shoe before it sank further in the quicksand clay and turned to stone. Grabbing the ruined loafers, they kept running toward the ruins.

Her husband's head jerked toward a different direction. Because of her helmet, she didn't hear the muffled screams that he did. The beating rain and the car alarms drowned out all else. But she followed him to a collapsed house. The owner was yelling at a pile of rubble, presumably to his family underneath. Her husband joined the owner in frantically tossing plank after plank aside. As her husband came to this neighbor's aid, Laurel pointed towards her parents' home and sprinted in the same direction. She stumbled through the devastation, cutting through what used to be a house. She panted while her pounding heartbeat rose in her throat. All of her concentration was focused on reaching the corner of the block where she could see her parents' home. She dreaded the sight around the bend.

Laura-East Limestone 5:00 p.m.

Laura and her family gradually emerged from the basement. There were water puddles on the kitchen floor tiles but everything seemed fine except for a few missing roof shingles. It sure felt and sounded as if the tornado was in their bedrooms, ripping the house apart at the sinews. They were drawn outside to look at the neighborhood that used to occupy the field across the road. It looked as if a giant lawn mower had mowed the houses down. Part of the neighborhood's landscape landed in Laura's front yard. She and her husband raced to check on their immediate neighbors but stopped in their tracks. The giant Doppler radar ball that was mounted on Highway 72 was now in the place of their neighbor's house. The only other recognizable thing left standing in the open field was a refrigerator. On closer inspection, they discovered that the refrigerator was actually the neighbor's tornado shelter with tree branches draped across its front access. Laura's husband cleared the debris and the neighbors stumbled out of their tomb, thankful for daylight and air. The shelter first saved their lives, and then threatened to take their lives when it flooded with water. All shelters were not created equal. Those with an outward swinging door could trap victims inside when debris piled on top of the opening. Laura's neighbors were able to walk away thanks to one of several heroes that emerged on April 27th, 2011.

Laura suddenly remembered her dream again. It wasn't a dream at all. It was a real event. Her reality was fuzzy, what with the memories of her Grandma's home destroyed by the Guinn, AL tornado, the book *F5* she had just finished reading, and her own recurring nightmares. She recalled that in 1974, an identical tornado struck Madison County and within twenty minutes, another tornado followed behind it, killing rescuers and those who crept out of their shelters. It could happen again. Laura grabbed the children and made a run for their house. The long gravel drive turned into a never-ending tunnel that seemed to get longer and longer like in a movie. When they finally reached the front of the house, Laura's eye detected a flaw on the front façade. A gaping crack ran along the length of the bricked front, separating the house from the attached garage. Her house ripped apart after all. She crept back to the basement and stayed there.

Laurel-East Limestone 5:00 p.m.

Laurel trudged through unrecognizable debris on her mission to see about her parents. There was the house! While she did not see her parents, she saw one end of the house, then saw the other end. It was intact. That was all she needed to know. A great sense of relief flooded over her when she realized that her parents appeared to be fine. She ran back the way she came to help her husband and their neighbor. It was difficult to avoid the obstacles in the road as Laurel zigzagged between wires, wood, nails and shingles. One coiled wire wrapped around her boots and caused her to trip. She landed on the slippery asphalt, flat on her face. It seemed like forever that she lay in the road while the rain drenched her back. She was so overwhelmed and confused that she was oblivious to another tornado that was passing nearby. When Laurel finally stood shakily on her feet, she hobbled to where she last saw her husband. Her aching forehead made her realize that the horse helmet she was wearing probably saved her from serious injury and from spending the night on the street or in the hospital.

She would not soon forget the scene before her when she returned to her husband. He and their neighbor were lifting a washing machine overhead and tossing it in the dump pile while human hands were waving from below the rubble. They struggled to pull the family out from underneath the house remains. They pulled out a screaming woman who appeared to be in shock, and next, a child who was just as shaken. The woman had a gash across her thigh that bled and mixed with the rain, forming pink puddles as she was carried through the drainage ditch to the safety of Laurel's home. Laurel's husband sacrificed his muddied loafers and lent them to the barefoot neighbor. Upon reaching the garage, Laurel instinctively wiped her mud-covered boots on the doormat before entering. Once inside the kitchen, Laurel stood and watched as her neighbor's leg bled onto the kitchen floor. She couldn't help herself...it was difficult to shut off the housekeeper inside of Laurel. She reclaimed her children from the safe room and administered first aid to her neighbor. Her husband left the house to recheck on Laurel's parents, but returned much too early.

Almost as soon as her husband went out the door, he was back again. This time he was cradling Laurel's father. Her husband had found her father lying in a heap on their garage steps, too exhausted to take the final steps into his daughter's home. Laurel felt sick. She only wanted to ensure that her parents were okay. She didn't consider that they would do the same, concerned for her safety. Her dad almost didn't make it to her house.

Later that evening, because Laurel's mother had prepared a big dinner before the storm, the families ate like kings and queens with grilled marinated steak and freshly cut strawberries. These would be the only delicacies in the midst of the destruction. The exhausted heart, bruised forehead, destroyed house, injured leg, and traumatized kids would have to wait until after dinner.

Shelly Van Meter Miller

GENESIS

2
STARS FELL ON ALABAMA

Things fell on Alabama. A mustard colored blanket of pollen fell every spring and basted the entire state with an annual pat-down of barbecue-like rub. It coated everything from the cars on the road to the hairs in the nose. Our lungs heaved in and out like accordions to flush out the caked-on particles. If I didn't know better, I'd worry that the glowing particles were radioactive emissions from the nearby Browns Ferry Nuclear Power Plant. Like clockwork, the pollen showers happened every year during tax season. You could always count on pollen and taxes.

Occasionally other things fell to the ground with more impact than pollen pollution. Not many states could claim that stars fell on them, but Alabama did for years. I drove a vintage Volvo for what seemed like forever. This car was older than the internet. It came with a spoiler on the back and a license plate underneath that used to read, "Stars Fell on Alabama." The plates changed but my old faithful car did not, except for the inside cover on the ceiling. It was stapled so that we could see who else was riding in the same car with us. Not that everyone wanted it stapled. Riders sometimes preferred that no one else spied them as passengers inside this eyesore of a car that to our neighbors' dismay still decorates our driveway with a worth of negative five hundred dollars and counting. Unfortunately, we missed the window for the Cash for Clunkers program.

I remained curious about the 'Stars fell on Alabama' theme on the license plates. It would have been nice to know why I drove around the country claiming that stars fell on Alabama. While pumping gas, people from other states would inquire about the license plates. I was clueless. They'd mutter, "Don't you live in Alabama?" I realized that if Alabamians didn't know, then who did? I'd admit, "Well, I'm not from there." I had lived here nearly twenty-five years, and still couldn't claim that I was from here. I had always known that you didn't ever actually become Southern. You had to be born that way. Having been raised in Kentucky, I was as Southern as I could possibly get, transplanted to Madison, AL by my own free will. "Y'all" rolled off my tongue like honey and I had raised three daughters in the South. That should count for something. My daughters proudly accepted the "Grits" badge of honor to define themselves, a trademark standing for "Girls Raised in the South."

Huntsville, AL was better known as the Rocket City. Huntsville's claim to fame was in the space arena, so at first I believed the falling stars theme was connected with our Space and Rocket Center. A three hundred pound meteor was found in Selma, AL over one hundred years ago, but that couldn't be the reason either. In 1955, what was described as a 'star chunk' crashed through the roof of a home in Sylacauga, AL. The nine pound meteor fell on a woman while she was napping, bounced off the radio, and created a crater on the woman's leg.

The woman reported the incident to authorities. Officers tossed around the black, satiny rock then airlifted it to an Air Force base for further observation. When the woman's husband returned from work, he wanted a piece of the rock but found that it had been taken into custody. Hiring an attorney, he demanded the return of the star. It was released to him 'on bail.' The husband then stored it in a vault for safe keeping. It was the first modern occurrence of a piece of a star actually hitting a person. In 1911 a dog in Egypt was hit by a meteor. So besides Fido, Alabama was the only place where someone actually had a star scar.

A court case ensued between the actual owner of the house and the woman hit by the star in her rental home. It was a contest between the gaping roof hole and the gaping hole in the woman's leg for star ownership rights. The landlord claimed that the meteor fell on his property and was therefore, his property. The woman, demonstrating her bruise, argued that the meteor belonged to her because it fell into her lap. (Sunbonnet Soliloquy by Jewell Ellen

Smith) One could say she was star struck.

Spending the next several years birthing 'Grits,' I put aside the 'Stars Fell on Alabama' issue until I heard a song that reminded me of it again. Jimmy Buffet was crooning a tune, other than *Margaritaville*, called *Stars Fell on Alabama*. Not only did the historic event inspire several songs and remakes, entire books were written about it too. The 'Stars fell on Alabama' license plate had nothing to do with any of my guesses so far, although the Sylacauga, AL story was one of my favorites. Further research confirmed that I had to go all the way back to the night of November 12, 1833 to understand the stars theme.

As far as anyone knew, it was a normal night and most folks had gone to bed at their usual time. Some folks were out celebrating the annual holiday at Huntsville's Pulaski Pike Race Track with gambling, horseracing, and cock fights. Right before midnight, the card dealers were alarmed by sonic booms, patrons screaming, and dazzling bursts of light. They abandoned their posts and dove under chairs to shield themselves from a stunning, earth-shattering display in the night that could only be described as a major atmospheric disturbance like no other. Mass chaos ensued.

Those who weren't into the party scene, but had gone to bed early, awakened by the same numerous and intense rays of light in the middle of the night. We would liken it to a series of laser beams shining in our eyes intermittently. The flashing strobe lights caused the roosters to crow thinking that day had dawned. The roosters in those cock fights were uptight and confused as well. The entire town was in pandemonium, and the roosters' piercing cockle-doodle-dos added to the mayhem in the premature dawn.

Fearfully, farmers wiped the sleep from their eyes to squint at the fiery display. The entire town drifted outdoors to witness the pageant. If it had happened in this age, we would exclaim, "Wow!" "This Leonid's meteor shower is amazing, out of this world, the best I've ever seen!" But to nineteenth century Alabamians who weren't aware of the Galaxy of Leo's habit of raining down meteors periodically, they only had two words for this phenomenon: Judgment Day. For it is written in the Book of Mark 13:25-26, "The stars will fall from the sky, and the heavenly bodies will be shaken. At that time, people will see the Son of Man coming in clouds with great power and glory."(NIV)

In Angela Walton Raji's blog, she quoted stories from her great, great grandmother, Amanda Young, who was a slave when the stars fell in 1833:

"... We was all scared. Some of the folks was screamin', and some was prayin'. We all made so much noise, the white folks came out to see what was happenin'. They looked up and then they got scared, too. But then the white folks started callin' all the slaves together, and for no reason, they started tellin' some of the slaves who their mothers and fathers was, and who they'd been sold to and where they took em. The old folks was so glad to hear where their people went. They made sure we all knew what happened.........you see, they thought it was Judgment Day."

Undoubtedly stars were falling from the sky in great numbers, just like the Good Book said. The stars fell on Alabama at the rate of 10,000 stars in an hour! All eyes were peeled to the heavens, watching the clouds anxiously. It appeared that the sky was on fire and looked like the world was coming to an end. Every written record documented that no words could describe that night. Sky was ablaze, skyrockets exploded, fireballs soared, lights streaked across the sky, and stars rained down as bright messengers from the sky with flashes of light and the firmament in fiery commotion. These were some of the descriptions that the Patmos Papers "Falling of the Stars" prophecies used to describe the celestial phenomenon. If news reporters were to broadcast the story live today, they'd say, "You just had to be there."

This most spectacular display occurred in the southeastern United States in North Alabama. Both the partiers and purists were in the same boat as the stars rained on the good and the bad. Not only was nature putting on one of its finest performances, but those on earth were acting out an entertaining show as well. According to Donna Causey's "Stars Fell on Alabama" article in Alabama Pioneers, with so many stars falling, people believed that the Second Coming was at hand. Jesus could come any minute and some homes needed a good cleaning before His arrival. Folks dumped liquor and dice out the windows, intuitively knowing that Jesus wouldn't approve. They cracked open their Bibles and blew the dust off the covers. Travelers packed up and dashed home to their families for the Day of Judgment, not to be caught dead in someone else's liquor and dice-filled home that didn't belong to them. Besides, they had their own homes to sanctify.

The world did not end in 1833, but the night the stars fell had a profound effect on Alabama. It was the first time people had ever seen the sky raining stars. Because of the star downpour, the term "meteor shower" was coined. That November evening became a calendar marker for the next century. Townspeople dated everything based on either happening before the stars fell, or after they fell. It equated to our present day calendar marker of occurrence, before or after 9/11.

Much of the titles of our present-day events could be traced to the night the stars fell in 1833. Huntsville's annual festival of the Galaxy of Lights attested to our star fanaticism. The Huntsville Stars minor league baseball team made their home at Joe Davis Stadium, 'the Joe,' since 1985, proving that there were other sports in Alabama besides cock fighting. We had other sporting events such as Huntsville Havoc hockey, football, football, and more football.

Stars weren't the only things that fell on Alabama. Recently, a band of twisters dropped from the sky and collided with the earth. Just as football fever pounded in our warring blood, tornado terror pounded in our crimson mud. The tornadoes lined up as if in illegal formation and after many false starts and a two-minute warning, the field of play was leveled by intentional grounding. We were on the receiving end with the penalties stacked up against us. Although we huddled together, there was no neutral zone. Through a series of direct snaps and a sweep, we were sacked by tornado bombardments. The opponent was a master of trick play, and used an offensive aerial assault that crushed our safety and defense. By the fourth down of the twister game, we lost control of our homes and forfeited with a losing season.

Being good sportsmen, we coupled tornados with football and often clumped them together in the same story. Every stirring tornado tale somehow closed with the subject of National Championships, ending in, "Roll Tide," or "War Eagle." Both tornados and football were a part of our heritage, bringing us together, and tearing us apart at the same time. Whenever we heard, "Touchdown!" we instinctively cringed, not knowing whether it meant someone scored or that a tornado was spotted.

In 2011, Alabama added an additional epoch to the dates that changed life as we knew it: occurrences before April 27th or after. The day became Alabama's new century calendar marker, no longer referring to the stars falling as the divider. Some compared our 4/27/11 to 9/11. From the building structures crumbled to dust, to the outpouring of neighborly love, it was similar to what followed after America's own airplanes were used as weapons on September 11th. When our red dirt was stirred up, so was our good will. Ten years after September 11th, we still remembered the aftershocks and were reminded of them again when devastation struck aimlessly in the form of tornado torpedoes on April twenty-seventh.

More than one monster spawned from the clouds in April of 2011, but it wasn't a shower of stars, nor were they exploding airplanes flown by terrorists. Instead, a lethal cloudburst descended on our land and spawned a series of deadly tornados. The twister's mission seemed to search and destroy to the point of hunting down the same neighborhoods and businesses more than once. The face of Alabama changed in the blink of an eye. A deluge of windstorms terrorized citizens in its wake, hijacking many lives along the way. Chased into shelters and hiding out in safe rooms was a lifesaver for residents. Ironically, we feared the random tornados just as acutely as we feared random acts of terrorism. Tornadoes were weapons of mass destruction in our part of the country.

Alabama tornado paths trace back to the 1800's as well. Both tornadoes and stars fell on our soil at that time. The year 1884 marked the first deadly tornado in Alabama's state history, an F4 on today's scale. It was one of sixty tornadoes to bombard the Southeastern United States on a freakish February day. Because of the range of destruction, the tornado outbursts were later called the Enigma Outbreak, catching everyone by surprise in the middle of winter. When the 1884 tornadoes lowered themselves from the sky, they left 420 people dead. NOAA (National Oceanic Atmospheric Administration) ranked the outbreak in third place on their "Famous Large Tornado Outbreaks in the United States" study. North Alabama had two mass "Come to Jesus" events—a star storm and a tornado storm. No wonder citizens thought the world was ending. Unfortunately for many, this did mark the end of their world.

In "Sunbonnet Soliloquy," Jewel Ellen Smith explains how a storyteller could resurrect the stars tale: She would leave out the tornado part because it did not make a nice bedtime story. She would begin soothingly, "Once upon a time," when recalling the night the stars fell. Dreamily, she would continue in a sing-song voice while her audience marveled that the starry, starry night still holds a special place in Alabama folklore. She would close the story on the banks of Mobile, AL and drop to a soft whisper. When all were mesmerized by the tide kissing the shoreline, she would have them picture all the starfish along the coast. "You see, here lay many of the stars that drifted down from the sky in 1833. Now they have come to life and live in the sand by our sea. If you peer closely into the shimmering water, you can see the sea stars still twinkling," she might murmur gently. That was a nice story. And we all lived happily ever after. But not just yet.

Shelly Van Meter Miller

3
RUN MAMA RUN

The falling sky was not an issue for me. I was only afraid of a few things in Kindergarten: strangers, 'Bloody Bones,' dark closets, clouds that chased me, and spiders. Arachnophobia was self-explanatory. Strangers were somewhat trickier. Someone might be strange, yet not considered a stranger (most likely a relative), while a real stranger didn't look strange at all. I played it safe and stayed away from most grown-ups.

It was in Kindergarten that I became obsessed with 'Bloody Bones' ghost stories. Bloody Bones was a monster that lived in a cupboard under the stairs. He ate children who told lies or used bad words. Every tale ended with, "I'm Bloody Bones and I've come to take you away." The spooky stories trace back to the middle ages in 1550 and were written in the Oxford Dictionary at that time.

The gathering of Bloody Bones diehards during recess knew that our teacher, Sister Judy, didn't care for the gore. One of us would keep a lookout for her strolling past us during the Bloody Bones finale. As the storyteller, I rehashed the same tale over and over and built up the suspense. When Sister strained to overhear our hushed tones, we convinced her that we were discussing Dick and Jane. Forty years later while house hunting, my husband pointed out a pantry underneath the stairs as a possible tornado shelter. As if I would go under there after what I learned in Kindergarten! A story from the Middle Age would haunt me into my own middle age. Bloody Bones lived on.

My fear of dark closets had a little to do with 'Bloody Bones,' but mostly it was from the confessional. I never forgot the time that I waited in the church pew to confess the sins of a six-year old. Booths were on either side of a larger closet which had the priest inside. My class witnessed the priest entering the closet, sometimes catching his robes in the door. The scene was especially hilarious since we weren't supposed to laugh in church. That's why we thought the nuns were present, to act as ushers and laughter monitors.

I always wished school would dismiss before my turn. I prayed more about being saved by the bell instead of being saved from Hell. My turn came as I walked the line toward my first confession. I cracked the door open for a sliver of light but the nun extinguished it by securing the door shut behind me. I groped around in the blackness on hands and knees while searching for the kneeler, and could hear soft murmurings from the closet next to mine. My heart pounded loudly in my throat, my mouth dry as a desert. Suddenly the priest opened a sliding screen between the booths. The moving lips scared the confession out of me. Up flew the screen and I babbled on cue, "Bless me Father for I have…peed" The missing word was supposed to be, "sinned," but I felt a warm spray run down my legs and puddle around my kneeling knees. Not only had I sinned, I had peed in my pants.

Using the confessional as a bathroom still troubled me. I thought of it every time that a tornado siren sounded and my family was forced into a dark closet. Thunder caused the door to rattle on its hinges and sometimes we lost power. The dark chamber would remind me of a confessional. Thankfully during tornado warnings, our safe interior room happened to be a bathroom too.

On the last day of Kindergarten, we celebrated with a certificate of completion and the delivery of school pictures. We left school and drove to my Memaw's house. Memaw shared her home with my Papaw, but it was still just 'Memaw's house.' I was proud of my school portraits where I posed in a checkered gingham dress, holding a bouquet of fake flowers. My Memaw bought all the wallet-sized prints for me to keep.

On the way to her house, we encountered an uncommon traffic jam while on the country roads. The standstill lasted what seemed like an eternity although we were only two more miles away from my Memaw's house. I could only stand in the Volkswagen for so long.

Car seats were invented before I was born, but they may as well have been electric chairs because children refused to use them. I fought my brother for the little pull down cushion in the backseat. Car air conditioners must not have been invented yet, so my mother dealt with cranky kids while the vehicle warmed like an oven.

Drivers on the highway flagged our little Volkswagen around an accident involving a truck that had lost its tank which we saw lying in a ditch. We gaped at the wreckage and saw the tanker truck driver gesturing profusely, shaken but unhurt. I gave up tormenting my brother and became engrossed in my own portraits again, forgetting about the tanker.

My long, blonde hair was parted on one side with the other side tucked behind my ear. I shunned hair barrettes and thought that my right ear did a better job of keeping my hair out of my face. My Grandmother didn't think so. She pushed the barrettes on me while I swatted her hands away pleading, "I can see through my hair." Staring at the picture, maybe she had a point. One eye winked while the other one hid behind my poker-straight hair.

Once at Memaw's, we looked for dimes we could spend at the candy store. Memaw grabbed her pocketbook and dropped coins into our grubby hands so that we could purchase red hotdog gum and fake candy cigarettes. The chalky cigarette sticks crumbled to powder when we fought over the unbroken ones and snatched them from each other's grasp. I opted to smoke my portion of cigarettes in peace, while my brother Michael played outside with Cousin Tommy.

The boys were always noisy, but we noticed it more that day. The alarming commotion drew us outside to witness Michael and Tommy pawing at a vapor with a rake and pitchfork. The fog inched towards the house, consuming Memaw's row of purple irises. The Mimosa tree in the garden vanished in the murky haze. Paralyzed, I watched as the gas swallowed the mailbox and things disappeared, one thing at a time, including my brother.

A thick, gray fog enveloped us and we realized the fate of the overturned tank and its contents. It was an ammonia gas spill. I feared that the oncoming cloud was actually a tornado, forming right in my Memaw's garden. I'd seen black and white pictures of tornadoes in the Encyclopedia Britannica. As the cloud crept closer to the house, we attempted to outrun the blob. The air smelled foul and putrid. It stunk so badly that I could taste the acrid smell. I choked and gasped for fresh air that wasn't available. Covering my mouth with my sleeve, I found it even harder to breathe and pulled my pointed collar over my nose, but still no breathable air.

A hand wrenched my arm from its socket and the rest of my body complied as Mom dragged my brother and me toward the picket fence gate, the outline of which was barely visible. If the gate hadn't been startlingly white, we would have lost it in the gaseous fog. Stumbling after Mom, I approached the concrete wall that separated my Papaw's garden from the neighbor's yard. We always stayed away from the border although there was not a 'Beware of Dog' sign. There was no need for one. An intruder could hear the ominous growls and judge for himself that a vicious dog was penned inside. Mom hurled her children over the enclosure and I tried to scream but only a rasp escaped my throat. My tongue tasted the bitter gas and my eyes stung and burned. But that was not why I tried to scream. I worried that Mom had thrown us to the dogs. I waited to be torn like a rag doll, but nothing devoured me or even growled me to death. The fumes silenced the dog too.

We escaped to a neighbor's house where the air inside was breathable. The neighbor whisked us to the hospital but I could not see out the car windows. I wondered if I was blind. At the hospital, nurses ordered me to spit into a metal bedpan and wouldn't understand that I couldn't see. They just kept shoving a bedpan under my chin. I tried to tell them, but no audible sound came forth. I remember being most upset by not having my sight and unable to cry about it. My mother disappeared in a different ward because she was in her last trimester of pregnancy with my soon-to-be baby sister. I had never noticed that Mom was having another baby until then.

My brother Michael and I shared a hospital room. I could finally see through my clear tent, thanks to the nurse who administered eye drops to me, most likely taking her entire shift to do so. One time I kept a stinging bug in my eye for three days because I wouldn't allow the doctor to flip my eyelid. But I was over forty years old when that happened. Meanwhile, Michael was the boy in a plastic bubble, sleeping in his private oxygen tent. I guessed that it wasn't a good time to play our little game. Michael had cotton-top white hair. With hair so pretty, Mom kept his white curls until he was older. I pretended that Michael was a girl and named him Mary Ann, my favorite name. I'd whisper the title because Mom didn't like it when I called Michael by a girl's name.

I once embarrassed Mom while she shopped at Andersons, the downtown department store. Michael and I tested perfumes that smelled like Memaw's Rose petals while waiting for Mom to shop until we dropped. A sales clerk noticed two blondes circling the counters one too many times, maybe even smelled us first. I told her that our mother left us. She asked my name and then pointed to my brother, asking the same. I spoke for us both, "This is Mary Ann." The clerk inspected Michael's rugged clothes and Buster Brown shoes but he sure smelled like a girl. She announced in the microphone for the mother of Michelle and Mary Ann to claim her children at the second floor cash register. While at the hospital, I considered calling Michael, "Mary Ann."

Held in quarantine under the oxygen tents, the air was finally fresh although artificially produced. I left with my dad and came home from the hospital, but Mom and Michael weren't released as soon. Michael wrestled with the ammonia gas and was exposed longer to the toxic fumes, and Mom was seven months pregnant. Visitors mentioned that my mom was hurt while going over the concrete wall. Adults did not realize that just because I couldn't see, it didn't mean that I couldn't hear.

We got a lot of mileage from the ammonia episode. I used it as a teenager to get out of cleaning the bathtubs. I exited the bathroom while gagging and claimed that I couldn't bear the ammonia cleaner and the bad memories associated with it. My mother rolled her eyes at the trauma drama. I did suffer from bad dreams related to the spill. In my nightmares, the seeping gas was blacker and spun like a tornado. In reality, a tornado wasn't much different than a toxic gas and could suck the breath out of you too. When my tornado dreams finally faded, the real deal took its place.

4

THE PERFECT STORM

My childhood was exciting enough that I did not dwell on fictional tornadoes. Birthdays were a big deal, especially for our country. The United States prepared for its Bicentennial celebration years in advance. Two-hundred years was so old, I thought. Whether it was fashion, a Pin the Tail on the Donkey game, or a peace sign, everything was in a red/ white/ and blue theme. Teachers used to tell us that we were so lucky to participate in the 200th year birthday of our country because we would not be alive for its next big birthday, the 300th year celebration.

I was just like every other little girl in the seventies. I assembled Barbie Jets and swimming pools, and argued over who had to be Ken. Miniature pizzas made with Ragu spaghetti sauce and Betty Crocker doll-sized cupcakes flowed from Easy Bake ovens to share with friends. A mud pie was reserved for someone you didn't like.

I have fond memories of my old Kentucky home. For six years we lived in a trailer park across from the steel mill with railroad tracks practically in our backyard. Every time a train passed, the trailer lurched on its axles and my one goldfish shook when the water sloshed in his round fish bowl. Every train passing was an exciting event and we would stop whatever we were doing to wait for the caboose. Onboard, a train operator waved with one hand and barely hung onto the rails with the other. Clothes hanging on the line were air dried as a train flew past. The tracks were right behind my metal swing set. My first spanking was because I crept too close to those tracks.

I almost avoided my second spanking. Our trailer park had only a few straggly marigold flowers. My Memaw encouraged my love for flowers, so I would pick them on a whim. Just three trailers from where I lived, some colorful plastic flowers with pinwheels decorated an elderly lady's yard. I coveted them every time I rode my Schwinn bicycle past her trailer. One afternoon, I plucked every one of those twirling flowers out of the ground. I pitched them into my bicycle basket, kicked up the kickstand with a swift swipe, and my petite feet frantically pedaled. I replanted the fake flowers behind our trailer.

I couldn't believe the posse that banged on our door that evening during supper. The old lady led Charlie, the trailer park's head honcho, and another witness to accuse me of stealing. I hoped no one would notice the plastic petals flapping in the breeze nearby. I hid my dirty fingernails that did the digging and denied stealing the flowers. The old woman ripped her plastic plants out of my garden and waddled back to her trailer. My dad wanted to believe me until he glanced at my fingernails. That was my second spanking. Plus, I had to say, "Sorry, Charlie."

In 1974, Saturday mornings were reserved for cartoons. We channeled through the only three stations on our TV to find the show we wanted to watch, and we did this by walking to the television and twisting a channel knob. No one ventured out early on Saturday mornings not for Little League games, piano recitals, nor karate tournaments. Cartoons began at a decent hour so that we could sleep late. We had our choice of *Scooby-Doo*, *Shazam*, *Underdog*, or 'Hey, Hey, Hey it's *Fat Albert*. Adults were too busy being grouchy with Archie Bunker or hee-hawing over Hee Haw. They didn't mind that I watched too much TV even though they warned that too much television could make me blind.

We had the most fun at Miller's Lake. Once I sort of learned to swim, Aunt Charlotte invited me to Miller's Lake with her. The manmade beach had a genuine concession stand, sliding boards, and rafts with trapezes that swung into the water. We performed a jig to cross the scalding hot sidewalk to the changing rooms, maneuvering past teenagers grooving to Brownsville Station's *Smokin' in the Boy's Room* playing over the loud, scratchy speakers. I sang along with a melting push-up ice cream sliding down my chin and neck.

The relaxing days of the 1970's drifted by as we searched for four leaf clovers or made necklace chains from the purple henbit weeds. Our biggest concern was not making curfew, which was 'dark.' Unable to define exactly what dark meant, it was finally settled that we had to be indoors before the street lights came on. We walked many country miles to go anywhere, usually in massive snow drifts. Unlike our forefathers, we didn't walk barefooted. We sported the wooden Dr. Scholl's clogs on our feet. Life was uncomplicated, the way it was for children everywhere.

I love to reminisce the good times of the seventies, but I recall one scary time. I remember it as the day that the wind and whistles blew. Unfortunately it was an event that kids across thirteen states in the heartland would have in common. We would all share a similar nightmare. It began while we were at school. The weather was unseasonably warm and we had spring fever. We didn't anticipate tornadoes because common myths assured us that the hills surrounding our town would protect us from twisters as long as we stayed away from the Ohio River, since it was believed that tornadoes follow water.

I attended elementary school during 1974. We had recess daily and that was the only reason we cared one iota about the weather—to determine whether PE was in the gym or outdoors. During dangerous weather, we stayed inside the classroom and played a quiet game of 7-up at our desks. Much like dodge ball, you ducked your head and a player tapped you, usually slugged you, on your head. Your job was to guess who had smacked you. One day, the storms were so menacing that we played 7-up all afternoon and had to forego our cleaning routine of banging chalk erasers together outside. With the lashing winds and the rain coming down in heavy sheets, the outdoors all but disappeared. Suddenly all heads popped up when a crack of lightening caused the fluorescent lights to flicker and was followed by a thunder boom. Game over.

On that third day of April in 1974, children in several states: Kentucky, Indiana, Ohio, Mississippi, and Alabama had something in common. We were united in our fear of death and were afraid that we would be taken up by a tornado, straight into heaven. That afternoon, the heavens gave permission for this storm to come down to earth and take 330 lives with it, many of them children. The super outbreak of tornadoes was the second worst storm of that century. I remember exactly where I was during the stampede of tornadoes that day. I can even recollect the color of my knee socks because my kneecaps were pressed against my face.

The principal's voice shook over the PA system as she commanded students to precede single file into the interior hallway. We were escorted to the nuns' convent next door to the school, but not before each teacher blew a shrill whistle to herd us like cattle. We had practiced tornado drills before and were told to curl up into a ball with arms wrapped around our heads. This day, the teachers failed to reprimand the hall monitors for forgetting to check the bathrooms for stray students. Even the most conscientious monitor neglected his duties during all the commotion. Looking back, it would have been safer to ride out the storms in the bathroom stalls.

Other students opened the windows before assuming their safety positions and the tornado pose. It was believed that if the windows were cracked open, then a tornado couldn't crack them. This would prevent our school in Kentucky from lifting and dropping into another state, like Kansas. I pictured being surrounded by Munchkins and telling one of the nuns, "Sister, we're not in Kentucky anymore." We milked this myth while rushing to lift the window sashes during the height of extreme weather. The idea that air flowed better through vented windows and released pressure wasn't true. We were blown away by the real truth later in life.

The interior hallways were the usual locations for our monthly tornado drills and we were not to confuse these with the fire drills. This had happened before and we were punished for not exiting the building for a fire drill but had relaxed against the hall wall, waiting for something to burn. Therefore, loud whistles blew to designate the difference in a tornado drill. The teachers blasted the whistles intermittently into our eardrums as we passed them. We were rushed out but told not to hurry. The mismatched signals created more panic, like when someone tells you, no while nodding his head, yes. We knew that anytime teachers displayed a false sense of calm, something bad was about to happen.

The storms continued to pound our elementary school. It was difficult to understand what was happening with whistles puffing and kids holding their ears in agony from the penetrating sound of them, the shrillness striking every nerve. I joined the herd of students with bebop shoes clickety-clacking to the nuns' quarters. Our nun teachers were always in full nun attire, like Sally Field in *The Flying Nun*. As much as I enjoyed the TV show, this was one day that I did not want to see a nun fly.

Our only source of communication with the outside world was a transistor radio which announced that a tornado was on the ground. A tornado warning was issued because someone actually witnessed it and alerted the radio station with, "Incoming!" Inevitably, the school lost power and kids shrieked in the dark. The nuns were prepared with candles and always seemed to know who was causing a commotion. They had eyes in the back of their habits. The convent walls were made of stone-cold concrete, and I flinched away from them, not knowing if they were wet or just cold as ice. The candlelight caused shadows to flicker across the walls so that the nuns' habits loomed larger than life and appeared to be floating around the convent. It was better to have kept my eyes closed.

Peculiar thoughts raced through my head. I was interested in seeing where the nuns slept because I often wondered if nuns slept at all. I worried that I forgot to wear shorts under my uniform dress that day. Just the week before, the nuns broke out their rulers to measure skirt lengths. Girls were sent home if the hem rose more than two inches above the knee. I made it through the previous week without growing, so I was probably okay on my knees for the potential tornado.

I still pictured a tornado as a smoke monster, much like the ammonia incident three years before. Only my imagination grew stronger by third grade, so by then I visualized a twister barreling toward me instead of slowly reaching a claw of gaseous smoke to strike me. I wished for my mom to grab my hand and whisk me away again like she did during the ammonia fumes incident. That was the last time that I ran from a cloud and I ended up in the hospital. I did not want to be in a dark convent with wailing students and numerous nuns chanting the rosary at different intervals. Situations like these were probably where the statement, "You'd better say your Hail Marys" came from.

Mumbled prayers reminded me of my own little sister who aspired to become a nun when she grew up. While I waited for something bad to happen, my thoughts went back to the room I shared with my two younger sisters. The youngest sister recited her nightly prayers aloud, blessing everyone that had been born. The Bible called it, "Prayer without ceasing." One night I asked my sister to say her prayers to herself. Soft sobs came from the bottom bunk. "What's the matter now?" I bellowed.

She whimpered, "Prayers to myself. (sniff, sniff) Why can't I say them to God?"

Meanwhile, the nuns' invocations became more insistent, but I didn't dare ask them to say their prayers to themselves. There were times in my life that I did not want to be where I was. Looking back, I found that the safest place was right smack in the middle of my misery and I just didn't realize it at the time. At the same moment that I was huddled in a convent, hundreds of other Kentucky children and those from twelve other states, including Alabama, were hunkered down, fighting for their lives during what would later be called the Super Tornado Outbreak of 1974.

Without an early warning system, more lives were lost. The tornado warning system of the 1970's was a step above Paul Revere's midnight ride with signaling flashes of lantern light. The only warning of an incoming tornado might be the funnel itself, shrouded in a black cloud and only visible with flashes of lightening. Many times the tornadoes wrapped themselves in rain and were undetected until the telling aftermath.

Evidently the Hail Marys worked for us because we all made it through those early tornadoes. I never knew anyone that didn't survive a tornado's wrath until I moved to Alabama. The 1974 breakout was the first I had ever known of a tornado or band of tornadoes to torment my town of Owensboro, KY. Our city was spared from the funnels that April day, but nearby towns, especially Brandenburg, KY was devastated and not spared at all. The National Weather Service in Louisville, KY noted that as the F5 tornadoes plowed through neighboring counties, there was a noticeable rise and fall of the Ohio River as water was displaced. The river bordered five states, so it would take a mighty force to alter water levels in a mere matter of minutes. A river tsunami seemed unfathomable.

Nobody knew what an F5 tornado was capable of, nor had ever heard the term. The Fujita scale for rating a tornado's intensity and damage was first introduced in 1971, but wasn't actually used until after the devastating tornadoes of April 3, 1974. From that day forward, the country knew what an F5 tornado was, after surviving six of them in one day. The speed of the F5 winds topped 300 miles per hour. The tornadoes on that day came from the same family, a single storm cell which spawned most of those tornadoes that swarmed over our nation. They dropped wherever they pleased and when the pillar of cloud made contact with the ground, it pummeled the earth relentlessly for hours.

For the first time in history, entire states were under a tornado warning. In Kentucky, our town of Owensboro didn't operate a warning siren, only larger cities like Louisville did. Louisville was one of the cities terrorized that day, and their radar screens actually saw the devastation coming in the form of green blobs preparing to attack the city. Radars could only detect solid objects, so there was no way to distinguish rotation unless you saw it with the naked eye. Tornado alarms were called 'air raid sirens' stemming from radars developed during World War II to intercept enemy aircraft. The tornado outbreak was certainly an air raid.

When tornadoes touched down, they scattered shrapnel across state borders. I discovered from Wikipedia's "Super Outbreak" that ninety-nine buildings on Redstone Arsenal were destroyed in my future home of Huntsville, AL. One of those was the Nuclear Weapons Training School. For months afterwards, classified documents were returned to the Arsenal by farmers as far away as Tennessee. Another nuclear facility located just outside of Huntsville, the Browns Ferry Nuclear Power Plant, automatically powered reactors down when nearby power lines were damaged during the 1974 storms. This would not be the facility's last time to shut down as a precaution to avoid a meltdown.

Alabama suffered immensely from the tornado outbreak. Some neighborhoods were hit twice within twenty minutes. It was one of the only states to have two F5 tornadoes in the same day. Wind speeds reached 300 miles per hour, with one tornado on the ground for over an hour, thus sealing the fate of many Alabama citizens. Pavement disappeared from roadways where the tornado rippled like an earthquake. People were struck down while in their church pews for Wednesday night services. Church members watched in horror as their deacons died when the walls tumbled down like Jericho. The small Alabama town of Tanner lay in wait for the waterspout tornado crossing the Tennessee River to take it away. Most of the town disappeared off the map, including two hundred mobile homes. The rising death toll would only increase as the day went on.

The longest recorded tornado in Alabama maintained ground

contact for almost two and a half hours, unstoppable until it reached Tennessee. The total combined path of all the tornados of that fateful day totaled 2,600 miles of devastation. What a nightmare! The terror was mostly during the night. The tirade of tornados stole our loved ones, our land, and our identity. We had never fathomed such utter destruction.

NOAA's scientists did. The science behind what was later labeled as the Super Tornado Outbreak of 1974 explained the weather phenomenon in layman's terms: A cold air mass came down from Canada and met with a warm air mass from the Gulf of Mexico. Typically, when Canada's cold air hits the warm moist air from the Gulf, air patterns tumble over one another to create the vortexes called tornadoes. That in itself is not unusual, the predictable way in which tornadoes usually form. A cold air mass clashes with a warm one and they dance together, forming rotation.

On April 3, 1974, the upper dry air mass was especially large and acted like a lid on the surface moist air. Moist air naturally rises to form normal thunderstorms, but with such an enormous cap that day, the surface air couldn't break through. Plus the dry air mass pressed down heavily on the surface air. This unseasonably warm day, the sun baked the air masses throughout the afternoon, causing a solar heating and the surface air to rise further, still having nowhere to go. Eventually, the surface air punched through the dry air mass lid, with friction and rotation. Both masses were equally powerful with uncontainable energy.

A super tornado outbreak with 150 tornadoes spawned and marched across the country, even into Canada. The perfect storm was rare and would not have occurred in its intensity if any of the factors were left out. The storm combined the worst conditions at the worst time. Scientists predicted that it was such a rare occurrence and would not befall again for another 100-500 years. But nature begged to differ and meteorologists would be sadly mistaken about the weather's future in another not-so-distant April.

The April 1974 Super Outbreak united children from different states. If you asked someone who was a child in Alabama on that April afternoon, they'd remember sitting along a brick wall singing, *Bad, Bad, Leroy Brown* by Jim Croce during the power outage. Kentucky children remembered it the same way. We would never forget where we were or what we were doing on that momentous day. Children across America were much the same in 1974. Although I weathered the same storm in Kentucky, my experience was identical to my counterparts in Alabama. School was out when it wasn't supposed to be, and that was something that kids didn't usually forget. We'd chant: "School's out, school's out, teachers let the monkeys out. One went east, one went west…" and I didn't remember the rest. But I never forgot that day.

Shelly Van Meter Miller

5
BARNSTORMER

Years passed and I put the convent experience behind me. While still a child, I never hid under the covers when I was scared. A clear view of the bedroom door was crucial to dread what was coming. It was a stare-down between the door and me. My anxiety caused the door to wave back and forth on its own, but thankfully my worst fears never appeared. All the same, I liked to know what was coming. Others felt the same or why else would they rush outside in the middle of a tornado warning to watch? The worst would be a tornado at night. Its distinctive roar would grab your attention and you'd feel compelled to gape at the big, black monster as it approached. I had never seen a tornado approaching in the night, but those who did would tell you that they'd rather not witness a massive twister accelerating towards them.

My Aunt Mary was one of the those who survived a direct hit from a tornado. She lived alone in the Kentucky countryside, surrounded by acres of corn tassels baking in the sun, and a once thriving pig farm with hogs bigger than a Volkswagen. I knew this to be true because carcasses of rusted automobiles, minus the wheels, were laid to rest in the same open field as the pigs. Once those hogs waded into the mucky pond, Cousin Pam and I sought an opening in the barbed wire fence of the pigpen and pretended to drive the horseless carriage across the field. Then we'd dart to the vintage car and squeal like a pig when we'd run into a giant porker lying inside the capsule of the vehicle. Its obnoxious snorts were enough to keep us at bay, but I noticed that the sprawled pig took up the entire length of the corroded car.

An old outhouse was preserved on the property which thrilled us to throw open the half-hinged door to exclaim, "Eeww!" The barn next to it lured us inside with dried tobacco hanging from its rafters and an old screech owl nested in the eaves. We packed as much play into two hours as we could while Aunt Mary watched her soaps, *All My Children* and *General Hospital.* Antique Schwinn bicycles, the kind with brakes on the pedals and springs on the seat, steered us down the gravel lane to a spot where we could best taunt the pigs and pick cattails out of a soggy ditch. Never mind why the ditch was soggy, so close to the swine. This was always a truth or dare moment because it was very close to the neighbor's land and their vicious dogs paid no attention to property lines. The first bark was the head-start we needed to retreat on our bikes, but fleeing on gravel meant spinning our wheels. We'd fling the bikes in the ditch and tear off to the nearest shelter, running recklessly into the outhouse, "Eeww!"

The farm originally belonged to my great grandmother, Rosie Mama. She lived on the homestead until she was ninety-eight years old. Her farmhouse kitchen table in which she used to slaughter the pigs was passed down to me. You wouldn't know that it's the same table now with the beautiful oak wood finish, but the bow in the middle where the hogs were laid on the chopping block hints of the table's past. I mourned Wilbur of *Charlotte's Web*, but then remembered the giant snouts inside the rusty automobile and realized that these were not storybook piglets. The scary pigs were anything but humble. During supper, the table was a good conversation starter or ender, depending on whether you lost your appetite while eating pork chops and applesauce.

Aunt Mary's three brothers worked the corn and tobacco fields on the property, but she survived all of them. The once flourishing land seemed isolated and lonely with no one to care for except the stray cats. Having no children of her own, Aunt Mary entertained nieces and nephews at her farmhouse. A simple shoebox kept us occupied while she cooked dinner. Inside the box, a dozen baby chicks huddled until they roamed the linoleum floor, venturing in and out of the box. We kept count to make sure they all made it back in the box. Naming the chicks didn't help with the gathering.

If we ate our vegetables, an even bigger surprise awaited us. After wheeling and dealing, I ate all of my cousin's tomatoes and she ate my corn. I had a problem with corn, because that was what the pigs ate. There was an entire silo of corn next to the pigpen. Eventually, the hand-cranked mixer for making homemade ice cream would make its way to the table. It was nothing short of magic that rock salt and elbow grease made creamy vanilla ice cream which Aunt Mary called custard. The day was concluded on the shady front porch overlooking the orchard while rocking in the metal glider with Aunt Mary and her handmade quilts. The fresh outdoors and the hard work of play made us bone-tired. Somehow I think that was Aunt Mary's plan. We snoozed on the pull-out couch under the open window and watched bugs nose-dive at the screen, trying to sleep with us. It was the perfect end to a perfect day.

We had all the entertainment that we needed, but two areas of the farm were off limits. The first was the watering well. The one time that I strayed near the hole in the ground, my Rosie Mama, who wouldn't lift her hand to hurt a flea, spanked me. Adults would 'send us into next week' if we had shown any fascination with the well. In Midland, Texas, Baby Jessica McClure was made famous when she fell into a well as America's captive audience sat glued to their televisions to watch the daring rescue two days later of the eighteen month old baby. Baby Jessica could've been me. But if I had fallen into the well, I would have been just as afraid of the punishment after being pulled out. Forget the 1-2-3 counting thing. Don't go near the well, "or else!" was the threat and "because I said so!" was the reason.

My generation never got the benefit of a time-out. There was no such thing, but there was such a thing as a good whoopin' with a convenient willow tree branch. As a result, when I grew up I swore to never plant a willow in my yard. I forgot to tell my husband about my tree fetish, so a willow tree was the first living thing planted in our first home's barren yard. I didn't know how it mysteriously died. Willows weren't required for behavior enforcement however. The once-a-year St. Martin's picnic haunted me all year long whenever I won the ring-toss game and brought home a wooden paddle prize, one with the orange rubber ball attached. The paddle ball detached with one tug and a new weapon was formed. I should've stuck with the cake walk, Bingo, and the yummy homemade burgoo.

The storm cellar was another no-no. The metal bolts on the swinging doors were unnecessary because there was no way I was going down there anyway. Cousins dared me but I'd rather dig a hole to China. There was always something more enticing around the farm, like running from angry dogs or taunting the pigs. I did sit atop the cellar doors when they were bolted shut, and played the *Say, Say O Playmate* clapping game with my cousin. I never saw anyone venture inside the cellar's black hole, but I assumed they did since there were layers of Mason canning jars inside. I envisioned a black widow spider guarding each jar of pickled beets. There was nothing scarier than that, except maybe a tornado at night. It would be a desperate decision to fling the cellar doors open and jump into the underground pit. The choice was between a black creepy-crawler and a black funnel cloud chasing me.

The glory days of Aunt Mary's farm waned over the years and Aunt Mary was alone at the ripe age of ninety. The chickens flew the coop and the pigs were somebody's bacon, maybe even mine and I just didn't know it. Aunt Mary kept to herself, hardly gracing society with an appearance, except for her clockwork stroll down the winding lane to retrieve the mail. She knew when visitors arrived because of the unmistakable grinding of gravel underneath the cars as they neared the kissing gate. My aunt still slept with the window cracked, listening to the symphonic, country night noises of crickets chirping, cats caterwauling, and the lone peacock across the road crying for a mate. Familiar sounds were comforting, the country's white noise.

I wondered if Aunt Mary heard the unnatural rumbling the night the tornado vacuumed her house. The unwelcome visitor grinded down the gravel lane and left an ugly scar on the peaceful heartland. It was near midnight when a funnel cloud untethered from the sky, screeching and splintering as it collided with earth. Aunt Mary must have felt the ground shake as if a freight train derailed and crashed into her living room. The unyielding tornado crossed paths with her house and something had to give. It would be the house. The century-old house was merely cast aside with the rest of the farm.

Aunt Mary lived to tell, but she didn't tell us anything. It was an alarming call from her distant neighbor who found her huddled on his front porch with a gash across her face. She appeared somewhere in the early morning, disoriented and in shock. We wondered if the tornado dropped her on his doorstep. It hurt us to think of her struggling through the night to seek shelter. We never knew if the storm cellar was put to use. After the tornado penetrated the floorboards, we stared through the abyss, straight down into the cellar. My aunt may have tried to find her way back home, but didn't recognize her own house after the devastation. We made sure that Aunt Mary never lived alone again, despite the fact that she was homeless.

At daybreak, our eyes performed a quick scan, but nothing made sense. Tornado aftermath resembled mixed Play-Doh colors, a murky, brown blob. Every object sucked through the tornado became the lump sum of rubble. It reminded me of a dumpsite. Gone were the hundred year old trees, including the apricot tree, the only one that I knew existed in the world. That might have been the tree that crashed through the front window and deposited itself on the couch where we had enjoyed our slumber parties.

Barn-raising literally meant that the barn actually was raised off the ground. We could no longer prove to our own children that there ever was such a thing as an outhouse because it, too, was gone. Gone was the same word we mouthed repeatedly, the same word that Aunt Mary mumbled over and over. FEMA was a new word. It was before Hurricane Katrina, so FEMA brought no preconceived visions of blue tarps. My mother mentioned that FEMA was coming and I asked, "FEMA who?"

The skeleton of Aunt Mary's house resembled the crooked house attraction at the old Opryland theme park. Opryland also had a ride in the clouds called the Barnstormer, and this was more like it. Like staring through a funhouse mirror, everything was distorted--convex and concaved, but mostly caved in. It was no longer the place to rock on the porch glider and sip iced tea from a Mason jar. However distorted the house, I investigated what was left of it before its appointment with the wrecking ball. I entered the halfway house, only half of it was standing now, and threw caution to the wind since the wind had taken everything else. I was attracted to Aunt Mary's spiral staircase. Thanks to the tornado, her original staircase was warped into a spiral with stairs that beckoned you to take the dizzying climb. The walls slanted at odd angles and suddenly the shell of the house groaned when my weight shifted. I chickened out and skipped down the lopsided stairs, grateful to be on solid ground. Unfortunately, this would not be the last condemned house that I would tiptoe through.

In the middle of the heap in Aunt Mary's yard, one item did not fit the horror picture. In a blender everything turns to mush, but then a complete chunk of ice surfaces. That was how it was with the towering, antique wardrobe that stood unscathed behind a mound of debris. My eyes riveted to the old fashioned mirror attached to the front, intact without a scratch. In its reflection were giant junk piles, amplified when sunlight ricocheted off the mirror. The wardrobe now stands in my own great room and I joke that it could become my tornado shelter. On second thought, black widows prefer dark closets.

If a stranger drove past Aunt Mary's land, he would never imagine that a one hundred year old farmhouse existed there. Once the house was torn down, its foundation of massive logs were hauled away and used to build a modern log cabin. The grapevine that used to climb over the picket fence still thought that it had a job to do. It wandered aimlessly around old bricks and tried to find a new purpose. Life moved on, mowing over the past. The tornado plowed everything but the corn fields and the memories. My heart swelled when I thought of the land forever changed, but more than anything, I longed for the lifestyle that vanished with it. Oh well, there was still the well.

6
CLASSIFIED

During the 1980's I received a tornado reprieve. No tornadoes came near my town or school for almost a decade. Our only concern was big hair--the bigger the hair the closer to God. Plus we thought a bobble head of big hair made you look skinnier. I regularly plastered my hair with an AquaNet hairspray can, which coincidentally was the same timeframe that a hole was discovered in the ozone layer.

Our slumber parties came alive with the game, 'Light as a feather, and stiff as a board,' or reading smuggled Judy Blume books banned from the school library. Watermelons and grapes still had seeds that you could spit. We wore Chinos, Bobby Brooks pants, and Izod sportswear with a cute alligator logo. We were entertained with Pacman and the Rubik's Cube. Yellow hostage ribbons surrounded our trees. I worked out with Jane Fonda aerobics, and knew whose phone number was 867-5309. I skipped school to watch Luke and Laura's wedding on General Hospital, and stayed up late to see who shot J.R. The Fonz impressed me with, "Aayyy," but Vinnie Barbarino from Welcome Back, Kotter didn't have to say a word. Michael Jackson was King of Pop, and the USA dominated the Summer Olympics when the USSR boycotted them. Every time America won a gold medal, we swung through the drive-thru at McDonalds for free: "two all-beef patties, special sauce, lettuce, cheese, pickles, onions on a sesame seed bun."

I attended Murray State University in the late eighties. My first

49

freshman week, the girls in the dorm pawed over a calendar with pictures of campus hunks. I especially liked January's flavor of the month who wore a tux jacket, a cute bowtie and a smile. Later while waiting for my date in the courtyard of Murray's Faculty Hall, I accidently sat across from a good looking guy who also waited for his date. He was none other than Mr. January and he had me at "Hello." Our eyes met and we were oblivious to our dates' arrivals. However, some things can't be rushed. This was the first time I locked eyes with my future spouse.

My college roommate graduated and moved to Huntsville, Alabama. I had never heard of Huntsville before then. The only thing that I had in common with folks in Alabama was that I lived through the same tornado outbreak in 1974 that they did. My husband once asked, "Didn't you always want to live in Alabama?" No, I only planned to visit my roommate in Alabama but never dreamed that it would someday be my home.

After college graduation my best friend and I moved to the nation's capital and interned for a United States Senator. We lived in a soon-to-be condemned tenement apartment and scrounged for coins to take the Metro to work, even shaking the couch cushions looking for stray change. We attended Sunday school for the free donuts searching for 'soul' food. Although we weren't rich, we were enriched by the culture around us. We were even invited as special guests to the White House.

A mutual friend interned with the Secret Service to detail an area in advance of the president's arrival. We would tease, "Where's the President going to be tomorrow?" but our friend never gave up the location, in which case he would have to kill us, he teased back. There was one occasion when he did want to kill us. It was the time he surprised us with special passes to the White House to see President Ronald Reagan returning from a trip. We received backyard passes to see the president and promised to be on our best behavior.

We waited on the White House lawn for the president to land as two helicopters emerged from behind the Washington Monument. One was a decoy and flew off before the real one containing the president approached the tarmac. In our anticipation, I happened to see an oval-shaped office, and leapt with excitement when I realized that it was the Oval Office. As the helicopter was landing, I moved to snap a picture of the landmark. I overstepped a chain link path guide.

With my eyes focused through the viewfinder, I felt myself being airlifted. The Oval Office swiftly fell out of view and the sky appeared.

Two secret servicemen had ambushed me. They jumped from the surrounding bushes and hoisted me off the ground with my feet dangling. A trap door opened underneath me and another agent swiped my camera. The guards exposed my film and reprimanded me in front of the other special guests. With my feet on the ground again, I lost my front row vantage point and slinked to the back. Still no president. The press was informed that Mr. Reagan was quarantined in his helicopter because of a security breach. That was me.

Eventually the president strolled up the White House lawn like he owned it. I lifted my chin above all the heads and shoulders and followed the president with my eyes. My muscles did not flinch while servicemen guarded me. President Reagan paused as doors were opened for him. He pointed back at me and my friend shrieked, "He winked at you!" I was the envy of all the guests. Only Ronald Reagan could turn a fiasco into something worth bragging about decades later. President Reagan winked at me!

The internship neared completion and it was time to find that "real" job before the Secret Service put me on a special watch list. I joined a job conference at the Willard Hotel in Washington, but not as a paying participant. I wore a handmade nametag to hobnob in the conference lobby with the recruiters, an idea I borrowed from Ulysses S. Grant. When he was president, his wife forbade him to smoke strong cigars on the White House premises, so Grant ambled across the street to the Willard hotel lobby to smoke in peace. The locals heard that Grant frequented the lobby and paid him unofficial visits, bending his ear, as my Grandmother would say. Hence the term, lobbyist, was coined from Grant seeking smoking asylum. I used the same lobby to lobby for a job.

I spread the classified ads across the hotel lobby's table, and had the same feeling that I got when someone was cheating off me in school. In fact, a man was hovering over my shoulder. While I circled job prospects with red ink, the same man chuckled. He beamed, "I remember doing that." Then he flicked a business card across the table. Underneath his company logo, "President" was printed boldly underneath. Obviously he wasn't the famous one who winked at me, but I did note that his business was located in Huntsville, Alabama. That was the second time that Huntsville, or "Huntsvul" as he pronounced it, appeared on my radar.

When I visited my girlfriend in Huntsville, I called upon Mr. Huntsville President for a summer job opening after retrieving his worn-out card from the bottom of my purse. He remembered the lobby girl and promised to review my resume. Never one to wait, I became anxious and interviewed at the Space and Rocket Center, the first landmark I saw on Governor's Drive. I was hired on the spot as a camp counselor and put to work an hour later, which was never a good sign. The kids ran circles around me in their miniature NASA outfits. The interviewer mistook my Kentucky accent and thought my college major was Space Communication instead of Speech Communication. I lasted two days on the job, never communicating with anyone. I would have tried harder if I had known that my near future would revolve around the space program.

Instead I planned a dinner interview with Mr. Huntsville President to discuss job prospects. Inside his car, he greeted me with, "Let's take a little ride." My stomach lurched, but not from hunger. His greeting sounded off my alarm bells and whistles. No sooner had I shut the car door before I began looking for a way out. We toured the soon-to-be Research Park with the many Bradford Pear trees already lining the streets, waiting for businesses to sprout alongside and for big storms to topple the trees. All the while, I got bad vibes from my tour guide and the night ended badly. Mr. Huntsville President had other ideas as to why I was so persistent, but I wasn't that desperate to find a job. It would have saved me some trouble if I remembered what I already learned in Kindergarten: Never talk to strangers.

Although the city tour turned into a complete debacle, I snatched a piece of Huntsville's history regarding a man named Wernher von Braun. Had von Braun still lived among us, he would be one hundred years old. His centennial birthday was recently celebrated, which speaks volumes about a legacy if a town celebrated a birthday without the birthday boy.

Von Braun's legacy was important to both Huntsville and our nation. Wernher von Braun was a young rocket scientist in Hitler's Nazi Germany, employed at a government facility which designed missiles during World War II. Von Braun was more interested in human flight, not human destruction. When the war ended, von Braun and his team of German scientists defected to the United States and spent the remainder of their lives launching Saturn rockets and landing them on the moon. Von Braun called Huntsville, AL his home and made Marshall Space Flight Center at the Redstone Arsenal his second home where his name would become synonymous with Huntsville's space program.

MSFC became NASA's hub for space flight. There, the Apollo missions transformed a dream into reality when America started asking "not what their country could do for them, but what they could do for their country." America was von Braun's country now but America was still lagging behind Russia's Sputnik program. Our German friends joked, "Russia beat America to space because their Germans were faster than America's Germans." In 1969, America asserted itself in the space race by taking one small step for man and one giant leap for mankind on the surface of the moon.

When the stars fell on Huntsville centuries ago, they foretold Huntsville's destiny. The city was destined to reach for those stars in return. The German defectors transformed the town from the cotton mouth of the South into a thriving, technological epicenter--a southern Silicon Valley. In a way, the Germans scientists were responsible for my relocating to Huntsville's Rocket City.

Shelly Van Meter Miller

VALLEY OF TORNADOES

7
VALLEY GIRL

"He said I talk like a Valley girl. And I said, like, whatever!" According to Webster's Learning Dictionary, I didn't fit the bill of a Valley girl who shopped until I dropped and talked nonsense until someone gagged me with a spoon. *Valley Girl* was a popular 80's song, but I wasn't that kind of a gal. I was about to become a real Valley girl, a Tennessee Valley girl.

It felt as if I had lived in Alabama my whole life, but I wasn't born and bred a debutant and never had a 'coming out' party. Being a Southern belle was difficult without attending a cotillion ball, so I was still considered a Yankee. I practiced my southern drawl as thick as sorghum molasses and transformed, 'y'all' into a two syllable word. I yearned to become a Southern lady, ASAP—"As Southern as Possible." But really it was the spiders that drove us to the South.

In 1989, I married my calendar boy. As soon as the honeymoon was over, my new husband and I moved to Sikeston, Missouri, home of Lambert's 'throwed' rolls. We gobbled 'throwed' rolls daily except when we frequented a little shack for raw oysters. After the oyster owner admitted that he got his shucked oysters "fresh out of Memphis," we went back to the 'throwed' rolls, oozing with dollops of molasses as our main dish.

The first day my husband left for work, I attempted to grow grass around our new duplex. Raised in the Bluegrass state of Kentucky, I was stumped that a plush lawn in Missouri didn't come naturally. It didn't have to be blue grass, just any grass would do. During my ritual of watering the dirt and growing mud, I sprayed a jet of water onto our square patio. A fuzzy cotton ball fell down at my feet, and on top of it, a shiny black spider with a cherry-red hourglass figure guarded her egg sac. She killed her mate for those babies and I just knew that the black widow would kill me too.

When I dropped the hose, it writhed like a green snake in the mud. I must have screamed loud enough for the teenager next door to hear me over the buzz of his lawn mower. The boy darted over to me in his cowboy boots. "Kill it!" I shrieked, pointing to the black blob. On my command, the teenager stomped the puff ball with the creature on top. Then we saw red—like red seed beads spilling and dispersing when a bracelet breaks. I stood barefoot in the dirt with knees knocking together while the teen blasted the hose at the red streaks. As if my worst fears couldn't get any worse, water ricocheted off a stack of bricks. Out of the brick holes, the flood of water flushed hundreds of black widows and egg sacs into the daylight. The teenager only saw four of them, he told my husband later, but I knew there were enough for an invasion. The widows won and I retreated. I begged to leave Missouri, nicknaming it, "Misery," and handed our duplex over to the spiders for their colonizing.

My husband landed a new job in Huntsville, AL of all places. He would surprise me one week after my arachnophobia event with a bouquet of flowers and a note that read, "Pack your bags Sweatheart!" I like to think he meant, "Sweetheart," and misspelled it in his excitement. We left Missouri and rolled into Alabama with nothing but our Malibu wheels since our chic black lacquer furniture went with the movers. We temporarily relocated to the Executive Lodge in Huntsville. My husband took a position with a NASA contractor, so it was the Space Shuttle program that was responsible for bringing us to the southern space town. That, and the pulled pork, collard greens, hush puppies and fried green tomatoes, not to mention the sweet tea and pickled okra.

The shuttle program had been grounded since the Challenger accident but was beginning a new day with upcoming launches on the horizon. America was ready for something good to happen in the Space Age. We were on the bubble with the Hubble telescope, and in the center of all the action. Business was booming for the Rocket City with office space at a premium. My husband worked in the 'bull pen,' an overcrowded room with cubicles on top of one another. Just like a Jubilee in Mobile Bay where there weren't enough nets to catch the fish, jobs were so plentiful with so much work and not enough hands to do it. Those were the days.

Good ole' Huntsville was the ideal place for us to land. The town loved its space program. The schools were named after shuttles and astronauts--Grissom, Discovery, and Challenger. Students in Huntsville learned to count, 5-4-3-2-1. Instead of zero, they would yell," lift off!" It was exciting living only thirty miles from the rest stop with a rocket ship on Interstate 65. You would think that my husband was slated for the next shuttle launch. I told everyone that he wasn't going up on the shuttle, but he would tell the astronauts what to do. He worked one of those first shuttle missions that put America back into orbit again. His first assignment was Space Lab-J, sending the first married couple into space. I was so proud of him. Huntsville was the place for space, out of this world, and an exciting place to live.

Cotton was king and fields encompassed us. We took detours into town as I squalled, "Honey, stop the car!" when we'd pass fields with cotton dangling on the plants. The roads were lined with it, paved with white strips on the shoulders. Anytime we would follow a cotton truck on its way to the gin, we watched it snow cotton. For years to come, it would be the closest thing we had to snowfall.

Downtown Huntsville was picturesque with Big Spring Park and Twickenham Village. The charming mansions were strewn with trailing Jackson vines woven across the wrap-around porches. The evergreen grew popular when Stonewall Jackson paid the ladies a visit during one winter of the Civil War. Wishing to make a lasting impression, tables were flocked with the only greenery available, a wild vine growing in the woods, nicknamed the "Jackson vine." It was a perfect pass-along plant among the gentry, and the only other way to attain it was to wait until someone died.

Twenty years later I went to a garden club sale which advertised Jackson vines for a bargain price. I tossed the spiny hunk of root and red dirt in my hands, picturing where I could use the climbing plant. As I pondered the possibilities, I overheard a distraught woman begging for a Jackson vine. She drove all the way from Scottsboro, AL and none were left except my chunk. I begrudgingly sacrificed my root and her eyes moistened in gratitude as if I had offered her a gold nugget. She choked back the tears and whispered that it reminded her of her mother. If you listen closely, the Jackson vine whispers its secrets of the South.

The city of Huntsville claimed more antebellum homes than anywhere in the state, but just two blocks away was a gothic fortress, a castle with a turret. Located in the heart of downtown, the bastion was complete with a moat from the Big Spring waterway encircling it. This was Huntsville's public library. Next door was a Baptist church with a larger-than-life-size painted mural of Jesus on the building. I overheard a child describe the church's mural as "the egg beater Jesus." Every time I drove past, I expected to see Jesus swirling round and round, stirring up souls. The glow of a startling, white cross nestled in the hilltop at Burritt Museum caught my eye. It towered over us as we came to the next intersection and nearly drove right into the Von Braun Center.

It did not take long to notice the clash between the past and the future in the Valley. The cotton fields, debutants and Jackson vines were not about to roll over and play dead to make way for change, technology and newcomers. If you weren't from here, you were a Yankee. I sought to fit in this land of cotillion balls and cotton balls. We moved to town at the peak of a power struggle between appreciating the preservation of the old South with its Confederate soldiers buried at Maple Hill and the modernization of new Huntsville with its Saturn rocket deposited as the monument on the Interstate leading to Huntsville. Looking at the cotton ball clouds passing over the cotton fields, the Space Center's rocket cut the scenery in half and looked like a giant Q-tip, shining in the sun.

Huntsville boasted two shopping malls. One was built in place of the one that was demolished by the 1974 Super Tornado Outbreak. Research Park was still a field of dreams, and Monte Sano Mountain rose to the east with its endless trails. The mountain was at the foothill of the Appalachians, but Alabama took what it could get, mountain-wise. From the mountaintop, a panoramic view included Jones Valley and the busy Airport Road. Our new valley was lush green with kudzu vines intertwined around high-tech missiles. Titanium white cotton fields pimpled the crimson red clay while the mountain loomed over the valley. We naively believed that the mountain would protect us from tornadoes, but we found that was just an old wives' tale.

8

SWEET HOME ALABAMA

We embraced Huntsville and made it our home. Much like the violent storms that plagued our state, the clash of classes and potpourri of people converged like opposite air masses, making life in the Tennessee Valley an exhilarating ride. The city served as a melting pot where north met south and city met county, military met civilian, and aerospace met debutante. Like many relocated transplants, we moved to the city of Madison on the outskirts of Huntsville. Huntsville natives considered Madison a cluster of cotton pickin' farms and were perplexed with its draw for newcomers. Over time the fields of snow had disappeared and were replaced by subdivisions and new high schools. Because of Madison's ever growing population, only one small cotton field remained, squeezed between Kohl's and the Outback Steakhouse on Highway 72.

The city of Athens was to the west. If you weren't in Athens, Huntsville, or Madison, you were considered a resident of the 'county' like Tanner, Limestone, Harvest, or Hazel Green. Birmingham considered anything north or south of them as 'county.' For years, Birmingham and Nashville conspired to ignore Huntsville as a bona fide city, failing to mention our metropolis located between them on their Interstate signs. Traveling along I-65, you could miss Huntsville altogether except for the giant rocket at the Welcome Center. We had the power to launch it if needed.

We liked Alabama but had some Southern lessons to learn. My

husband and I were anxious to fit in and went along with all things "Southern" in order to get along. Heaven forbid we remain Yankees while in the South. We had to start somewhere, so we started with proper dining etiquette. A waitress would saunter up to our table, "Whatcha gonna have to drink, Hon?" The correct answer was "Coke." When asked what kind of Coke, your next response might be, "Pepsi, please." And you always minded your manners with yes ma'am and no ma'am. It didn't matter if the waitress was ten years younger than you were.

Huntsville had two extremes. You were either this or that, and nothing in-between. I made a cheat sheet so that we could properly fit into Southern society and checked whether we were this…or that.

Either this…or That
Roll Tide … War Eagle
Big truck with "A" on trailer … mini-van with tiger tail sticking out of hatch
Southern Baptist … heathen
Football player … fantasy football player
Honor student … dog smarter than honor student
Natural blonde … fake blonde
Sell Mary Kay lipstick … only thing separating you from a pit bull was lipstick
Going fishing … gone fishing
Old money … no money
PTA … NRA
Wore a turtleneck … were a redneck
Whole wheat bagel … Krispy Kreme donut
Vacationed in Destin … spent vacation at the Talladega 500
Sweet Tea … Sweet Tea

Both sides were passionate about their positions and I wondered whether peaceful existence was possible. The obvious rivalry was Auburn vs. Alabama. If you were unsure of the other categories, this one was a mandatory decision and not a multiple choice. At first I did not care one way or the other and chose neither. It seemed insulting to choose none of the above. They were both the wrong answers the Saturday that I got my hair permed during the annual rivalry Iron Bowl game. Without an appointment, I walked directly into a hair salon and right into the barber's chair. I was the only customer. The stylist hurriedly threw some rollers in my hair and sat me under the big hair dryers. His plan was to check my hair after the perm had set. In the meantime, he would be "in the back" watching the

Alabama/Auburn football game. I sat and sat and sat. My perm set and set and set. It was half-time when the stylist remembered his only customer and I walked out of the beauty salon with a perm from H-E-double L.

I learned the hard way that nothing interfered with Alabama vs. Auburn game time. Merchants threatened to move the busiest shopping day of year, Black Friday, to a Saturday so that fans could watch the annual game. Alabama's economy suffered because of it. Finally both sides agreed to move the Iron Bowl to a Saturday. It was the only thing they could agree on. It was either that or move Thanksgiving.

The South, of all places, knew that a house divided could not stand. I wondered if our state of Alabama, or even our city of Huntsville, would ever come together and live in harmony. Then I saw it, or rather I heard it. The instant that Lynyrd Skynyrd's *Sweet Home Alabama* played, everyone stopped and practically saluted. Alabama was one in spirit for the duration of the song. The love for our sweet home of Alabama brought us together. If only the skies would remain so blue, like the song suggests. I saw a bumper sticker that summed it up: We love God, sweet tea, and the SEC (our football conference). We knew that as long as we all agreed on those three tenets, we would be okay.

We had no idea how exciting our Southern adventure would be. Most of it was like the downward spiral on a rollercoaster ride, while other aspects were more like being slung around a curve. Nothing was as surprising as when the ride accelerated out of control and the town turned upside-down within the first week of our move to Huntsville. We had never had a welcome like this before. And the sky wasn't so blue. It was definitely green.

Shelly Van Meter Miller

9
SNEAK ATTACK

T minus twenty-two years and counting. The saga began when we stepped across the Alabama border. A tornado watch was issued in November. I thought Bob Baron, the meteorologist, was kidding. Fall was at its peak and Thanksgiving was right around the corner. We were torn between whose family we would spend Thanksgiving dinner with, now that we were a married couple. Whoever heard of a tornado in November?

We were too preoccupied to take the watch seriously. There was nothing special about a tornado watch. There was nothing to watch. It only meant that weather conditions may or may not produce a tornado. Like my car's orange check engine light that burned out after three years of trying to grab my attention, a tornado watch was no cause for alarm. A tornado warning was different. I compared it to the red light that flashed on my dashboard panel which meant: pull over now!

The sky should've been ugly, but it wasn't. The color was an iridescent green and reflected on the University of Alabama in Huntsville's lake across the street. I remember staring at the pretty green sky while walking between buildings at Teledyne Brown, the company where I worked as a temporary employee, better known as a 'Kelly Girl.' Before email was used to communicate, I personally delivered important memos to other buildings on the work campus. When my boss called her colleague later to ask, "Did you get the memo?" she could assume that I had personally delivered the message.

I did not complain about my errands because it took time away from my photocopying position. Blinded by the light, I often needed a break from the copier's surging flashes. My diploma proved that I earned a college degree, but a photocopier position was the only job available for me after I flunked the typing test. Oh well, money was money whether I was making copies or making missiles.

Plus, the copy room's central location afforded me the best seat in the house. My cubicle faced a panoramic view of UAH's campus and lake. This photocopy girl and the president of Teledyne occupied large corner offices with the finest vantage points. Apparently the government thought so too, because the location later became home to the National Weather Service. We could have used the weather service during the fall of 1989 had we known what the sky had in store for us that day.

Those who remembered the '74 tornado outbreak that pounded Alabama would recognize the November sky. They would describe it as the same "sick green color," they saw before, but I didn't know any better because I was closed up in a convent in Kentucky at that time. In Kentucky we were used to bluegrass and blue skies. Huntsville's hazy shade of green sky didn't deter me from the lunch special at the old Ding How restaurant. Lunch in Huntsville began promptly at 11:00 a.m. If you were late, you may as well wait until dinner. There is a reason why Alabama has earned the title of the fourth fattest state in the nation.

Later that afternoon, the storms intensified on our way home from work--our temporary home, the Executive Lodge hotel. We wondered whether the weather would interfere with our dinner plans. Suddenly, the imaginary orange warning light burned bright red as the tornado watch formed into a tornado with no warning.

Even the weathermen were caught by surprise. The meteorologists learned of the tornado about the same time the victims did. A policeman from the K-9 unit called the news station when his squad car flipped upside-down. He visually confirmed that a tornado had touched down. It was an F4 tornado that eluded detection and weather instruments failed to spot. Bob Baron was the chief meteorologist on the air at one of Huntsville's three TV stations. He remembers scrambling when the officer called the station. Mr. Baron looked at all the fancy weather gadgets surrounding him and realized that none were actually tools that were of any use.

Around 4:30 p.m. on that Wednesday, damage reports began to filter in. My husband and I had no idea of the storm damage location because we had no idea where we were, still new to the area. I assumed that Madison was in Madison County. I assumed that Airport Road was near the airport, but was mistaken on that account. The harmony of emergency sirens was relentless near our hotel located off University Boulevard. Something was very much out of the ordinary. No damage near our hotel, we still got the inkling that bedlam lay in wait nearby. We decided to forego dinner and stay inside the lodge.

That night was a long harrowing one for Huntsville. It was an even longer morning after as the search for survivors continued. The tornado heaped hundreds of destroyed cars in piles as if ready for the junkyard. Most of the heaped cars had people in them. News reports were very grim.

Another myth was disproved that day. We believed that tornadoes were supposed to gravitate towards uninhabited fields, far out in the country. At the time of the November 1989 tornado's touchdown, Airport Road was one of the busiest streets within the thriving city limits. To make matters worse, a major contractor released its workforce early that day, adding even more traffic congestion to the area. The tornado descended at the onset of rush hour and most victims were either thrown from their vehicles or buried in them. Over half of the fatalities occurred in one major intersection.

A strip mall, doctor's offices, churches, schools and apartment complexes were situated on the busy road before they were leveled to the ground that day. The Waterford Square apartment complex was destroyed, taking additional lives. In all, eighteen Huntsville citizens lost their lives that afternoon and three more died within months from injuries sustained. According to NOAA's data, over 250 homes were tossed around in the tornado's fury, while eighty businesses were destroyed, causing over $250 million in damages.

Airport Road was in the heart of the Valley, but our mountain defense failed us. The land sandwiched between two foothills was steamrolled by the tornado in a very short period. All along, we were deceived with a false sense of protection that we thought the mountains gave us. The mountains still stood, but betrayed their valley. On Tornado Project Online, Dr. Bill McCaul dispelled common myths and quoted, "well-formed, mature tornadoes may actually stretch themselves into valleys and intensify. During this vortex stretching, the funnel diameter may shrink...causing the tornado to spin even more rapidly." According to McCaul, this was hardly what one would call protection for buildings located in a valley.

We experienced a jumble of emotions, grateful that our lives were spared while feeling a sense of loss for those whose lives were lost. It was a weak balance that teetered either way. As newcomers we felt like disconnected outsiders. It was disturbing to watch others mourn as we sympathized from a distance. There was a clear distinction between strangers and townspeople, helpless to change which group they belonged to, neither wishing to be in the other's shoes. It was a solemn time for Huntsville. So close to the holiday, it would make for a bittersweet Thanksgiving.

Meteorologist Bob Baron worked at the news station until 1:00 a.m. on November 15th, trying to get a better grasp of the extent of the tornado. As he drove home, he passed over Memorial Parkway and saw to his left, the devastation on Airport Road. Still without power, the area was black except for the bright lights of news cameras and the search-and-rescue spotlights that were focused on debris piles. Mr. Baron later found that two of his friends perished in the tornado as well as several acquaintances. In his own words, "It was devastating," he said. "I felt like a failure." In reality, his equipment had failed him.

As a result, more lives were lost. Nothing could have prevented the tornado from touching down where it did, but early detection could have saved some of those lives. The '89 tragedy was a defining moment in Bob Baron's life. Even for such a time as this, he could see God's hand. He vowed that never again would Huntsville be ambushed by another undetected tornado. Two months later, he formed his own company with a goal to save lives through weather science. If any good came from the deadly destruction, this was it.

I was not satisfied with labeling the ghastly tornado, "the tornado of '89." Hurricanes had names that once mentioned, evoked certain emotions. At the mention of Katrina, visions of a crowded stadium, jam-packed for the game of life comes to mind, along with muddy flood water, displaced animals, and runaway buses. A hurricane's projected path allowed time to name it as you tracked it. Something deadly deserved a name so that you could remember its destruction at the mention of its name. Tornadoes should be named if not before they approach, then after their wake.

Even years after the catastrophe, those that were "latch key" kids, home alone after school during the time of the tornado, still had psychological problems and were undergoing counseling for their fears. A routine tornado watch sent one of my aerobics students into hysterics. We heard the howl of the wind over the music as we cooled down to the last song. The student sobbed and later told the class that her mother was a victim buried in a car during the 1989 tornado. She had searched for her mother among the ruins, eventually identifying her by her feet. From then on, when it rained, the daughter's bad memories poured. A tornado was no longer a random, faceless misfortune; the tornado of '89 had a name, and its name was pain.

The stories of survival were just as prevalent as the stories of loss. The tornado had the potential to cause much more damage. Jones Valley elementary school was demolished, along with three churches nearby that were damaged. Had the tornado formed an hour earlier, children would have been in harm's way at the elementary school. Churches in the South regularly scheduled Wednesday night services and usually packed a full house. If the F4 tornado spiraled an hour later, church goers would have been caught up in the clouds.

An aerial view of the tornado damage showed Crestwood Hospital only a block away from the mayhem. The hospital tower was the highest point in the storm damaged corridor, but was untouched and its patients were safe. Some of the 463 injured victims were saved that evening by the hospital's proximity to the tornado ridden Airport Road. It would seem that stretchers could have rolled to the scene of the destruction faster than an ambulance could have carried the victims.

When witnesses saw the twister barreling down the busy road, they took shelter wherever they could find it. Customers at a bank rode out the storm in a bank vault. Shoppers in a jewelry store were protected by the only wall that did not collapse. A gas station attendant saved a girl's life by pulling her out of her seatbelt and dragging her into the station for cover. They were thrown from the building but survived. Another employee at the same gas station was thrown into the street and hit by a car. He survived with a broken arm. One lady was walking across the street and felt her dangling earrings lift into the air. She too survived.

Twenty two years after the fateful tornado of 1989, I waited on the same Airport Road for a dental appointment. It was exactly 4:35 p.m., the same time the F4 tornado surprised this town, decades before. The city sprawled again with bumper to bumper traffic and stoplights every three feet, it seemed. The strip mall was replaced by a TJ Maxx, while Panera Bread baked fresh bread next door, and Starbucks brewed coffee on the other side. I watched as children practiced soccer on a field squeezed between two churches that had been damaged in 1989. The oak trees were mighty again and offered an umbrella of shade over the road. Right after the tornado, workers had a difficult time chopping down the ragged remnants of trees that used to line the street. Chain link fences were wrapped around and embedded into the trees so that when volunteers used their chainsaws, it was metal against metal. As before, an arrow pointed toward Crestwood Hospital with "Emergency" printed on top. That one word evoked both relief and dread when you were in an actual emergency, but otherwise it went unnoticed.

On this November afternoon, the traffic crawled with cars, like a slow-moving slug inching up to curl over Jones Valley. Like the present drivers, the unaware motorists had nowhere to go, all those years ago. I wonder if they saw the tornado coming and tried to get away but couldn't. One man had driven over the top of the hill and met the face of the monster tornado, head-on. That was the last thing that he saw. I turned towards the intersection where the tornado victims had been. The intersection still claimed lives. I gazed upon two white crosses, a reminder of a hit and run accident where two teenagers were killed by an illegal immigrant. A chill washed over me as I pondered if there should be eighteen white crosses on that same corner to remember those who died on the fateful November day. I wondered too if my park bench upon which I waited was on hallowed ground.

The giant American flag snapped above me and canopied overhead. The flag pole clanged in the wind like a bell tolling. I watched the banner wave as if beckoning me to move on. While we should never forget, it wasn't healthy to relive old fears and dwell in the distant past. For many years, Huntsville mourned the painful anniversary of November 15, 1989 but experts believed it was unhealthy to commemorate death anniversaries after ten years. I frowned again at the busy intersection and then glanced back at the unwavering American flag. A nation of overcomers, time was supposed to heal all wounds—just so long as the tragedy never happened again.

Shelly Van Meter Miller

70

10

TORNADO ALLEY

T minus seventeen years and counting. I had lived a lie for years. I incorrectly believed that our suburb of Huntsville was located in tornado alley. According to the map, it wasn't official. Many citizens wished for a map revision to include Huntsville, AL as a corridor of tornado alley. But it did not take maps or labels to convince me that this valley was an alley. It took several lethal tornadoes and then I had no doubt.

I had believed that a meteorological entity composed the tornado maps. If tornadoes with the strongest EF5 rating, or more than one EF5 tornado on the same day were factors, Huntsville was already more than qualified to be in tornado alley. I had a bone to pick for the mislabeling of tornado ridden Alabama. But there was no such meteorological group with whom to argue. Tornado alley was simply a term that the media coined, and any ole' Joe could make up a name for his corner of the world. Someone tried to formally label our valley, "Dixie Alley," but it sounded like too much fun, as if tornadoes wound around each other asking, "Wanna dance?" while winds howled and trees hissed to the reverberating beat. Twin tornadoes were not as fun as Dixie Alley made them sound. Later the name changed to "Deadly Dixie Alley," a more definitive title. Regular people made up whatever name they chose for their tornado territory, so after experiencing repeated tornado warnings, I christened our nook in the Tennessee Valley, "Tornado Valley." My nickname for Huntsville has unfortunately lived up to its name.

When we arrived to Tornado Valley the same week as a tornado did, I became entrenched in the valley of tornadoes whether I wanted to or not. But with every new weather watch that didn't spawn a tornado, we relaxed and became lax. Sometimes we ignored the weather predictions altogether. We didn't throw caution to the wind, but we weren't as watchful as we should have been. We would stay in bed or peer out the window. "See anything?" as if we expected the tornado to knock and ask permission to enter. Bad weather was nothing to get uptight about. The warning sirens were almost considered normal. Sometimes the sirens sounded so often as if they were crying, "W-ooo-l-f!" But in the back of our minds, a little voice whispered, "This could be the one." Usually the thunder and rain drowned out that uncomfortable warning voice. Eventually, the unlikely happened right outside our doorstep and we were shocked and felt betrayed. We could not say that we were not forewarned.

Sun Lake apartments were used to stormy events, like when a lightning strike scorched the clubhouse right before we moved in. We believed the myth that lightning never strikes the same place twice. Some smart person said, "If something happened once, it would never happen again. But if it happened twice, it was sure to happen again." Lightening was up to its old tricks one stormy day as a severe storm passed through. We heard the sirens and jumped into the bathroom shower of our second story apartment unit. I shouted over the sirens for my husband to lead us in prayer. He began, "Bless us, Oh Lord, and these thy gifts, which we are about to receive…"

"Did you just say grace before the tornado?" I wanted to know. His lapse into the dinner prayer was the first thing that popped into his head. After the uneventful warning passed, we ate dinner, the food sufficiently blessed. The blessed tornado warning prompted my husband to search for that church home sooner than later.

We went from married without children to another phase overnight where conversations centered around potty training and whether babies should sleep on their backs or stomachs. The *What to Expect When You're Expecting* book by Heidi Murkoff became our Bible, but "sleeping like a baby" didn't mean anything to us because our babies never slept through the night. Many late nights we joined the neighbors on the patio to sing and play guitars, only stopping when we got to the Brady Bunch theme song. We gazed at the ancient stars and kept an eye on the Hale-Bopp comet. Tornadoes may have circled around us, but we missed them because we were in a fog from lack of sleep. Then once upon a time, all the babies slept through the night and that's when I started noticing the tornadoes swarming around us.

Or maybe it was Dan Satterfield who pointed out all the tornadoes. In 1994, Dan was the new kid in town, a chief meteorologist for the local weather station. He was a popular TV icon the same timeframe as Barney, the purple dinosaur that my kids obsessed over. The Barney show babysat my children for an hour each day although "St-u-u-pendous!" was repeated so often that I wanted a pillow to cover my ears. I gravitated towards the television whenever I heard Barney's closing words, "And remember that I love you." Suddenly, Barney's face changed into Dan Satterfield's. The next thing I knew, Dan was talking to my kids, telling them to grab their own pillows and get into the closet because a tornado was coming. Dan Satterfield unpacked his bags in the nick of time, right before an ugly F4 tornado.

My husband was a big fan of his (Dan, not Barney). He awaited Dan's presence in the Christmas parade, pretending he was waiting for the kids to see Santa. Dan gave my husband a wave from his convertible and my husband turned to leave, his evening fulfilled. I reminded him that we were there to see Santa's float at the end. You would think America's president had winked at him, or someone that important. I soon discovered that there cannot be two people in the same household who were weather aficionados. My husband studied tornado predictions, the Weather Channel, and Doppler radar. I would see a formidable cloud in the sky and declare, "Look at that wall cloud."

"That's just scud," my husband would say. I accused him of making up words. "How can you tell?" I pretended to still be interested.

"You can just tell," he'd answer back.

I was no closer to knowing what a wall cloud was. That was about the time that I took up snake hunting with a friend. Around Lake Edgewater, where the Sun Lake apartments were located, we counted sixty-seven different snakes but were unable to positively identify a single one of them. Some snake hunters we turned out to be. Even with picture charts, it was difficult to determine if the snake eyes were rounded or slits, or if the head was triangular or oval. We finally spied a cottonmouth slithering toward us with its head torqued at a ninety degree angle. We stampeded back across the boardwalk as it charged us and knew that it was a cottonmouth without waiting to see if the inside of its mouth was white as cotton before it struck. We could just tell. We could also tell that it was time to find a new pastime. So we took up alligator hunting off Greenbrier Road. But I digress...It was to be the same with wall clouds. You would know one if you saw one. Undoubtedly I would recognize a wall cloud without waiting for it to unleash its vortex before I could properly identify it. But that would be years down the road, one warm day in April.

It was mostly during the night when weather threatened our sleeping house. Extreme measures were taken to keep the babies asleep in their car seats propped in the bath tub during warnings. The tub became overcrowded as babies grew into toddlers and all their beloved stuffed animals joined us in our only shelter. As an avid scrap booker, every occasion was a Kodak moment featured in our family album. I even scrapbooked a tornado page with acid-free storm stickers around each photo of our family in the bath together, helmets and all. Tornado warnings were a regular part of our children's growing-up years and most of the close calls were documented in those scrapbooks.

There were times when warnings rang out but we weren't near our trusted tub. The ball pit at the McDonald's playground was not a good place to be during treacherous weather. It was hard enough to get the kids to leave the tunnels and slides, and sometimes it took tornado sirens to do the whistling for us. At the Madison McDonalds with a tornado brewing outside, I planned to locate the restaurant freezer and ride out the storm with the frozen Happy Meals. Before we ever met, my husband survived the 1982 deadly tornado that ripped through his hometown of Marion, IL while inside a McDonald's freezer. But my children and I would never see the inside of the McDonald's freezer in Madison because the manager wouldn't allow it. Thankfully we never saw the inside of the tornado either.

Sometimes tornadoes threatened to pay a visit in the early days of summer. While Vacation Bible Schools lured children with all the goldfish and gummy worms they could stand, or the chance to make an ocean in a bottle, tornadoes simmered, unbeknownst to us. By late afternoon when VBS playmates were invited over to play, either scud or wall clouds dotted the sky. The sirens would rev up and sometimes the new acquaintances would join us in our bath tub. Rub-a-dub-dub, I should've scrubbed before visitors jumped into my tub. The past ammonia cleaning excuses "didn't hold water" anymore.

Shelly Van Meter Miller

11
CHURCH PREY-ER

T minus seventeen years, one month and counting. "If you build, they will come," did not necessarily mean that people would come to church if one was built outside their back door. Churches dotted North Alabama, but despite their vast numbers, Huntsville was still considered one of the most "un-churched" cities in the Deep South. But revival was in the air. When the stars fell in 1833, citizens flocked to church to repent from sin. Revival was coming again to Huntsville, not because the stars were falling, but because tornadoes were.

When we moved to Huntsville, it was hard not to notice the tornadoes that fell from the sky. Henny Pennies cried, "The sky is falling!" And for some in my town, it did. I thanked my lucky stars the sky didn't crash through my roof, but many of my acquaintances were roofless because the sky descended upon them in funnel form. "Deliver us from tornadoes, Amen!" was a powerful enough prayer to lead believers to the Lord. The South had a long legacy of religious faith as well as regular tornadoes. The continual bombardment of tornadoes along with the Billy Graham Crusades could explain why so many churchgoers 'got saved.' In order to be saved, we needed something to be saved from.

Besides the Saturn rocket and snowy fields of cotton, churches were Huntsville's main landmarks. The downtown church steeples pierced the clouds. The nostalgic scenery enhanced the small town feeling and looked like a jigsaw puzzle backdrop. As we settled in the

South, "What's your name, and where are you from?" were the prime questions asked of us. The locals rendered the next question with utmost expectation: "Do you have a church home?"

"A *what* home?" I countered. In Kentucky, we didn't have church homes. In Alabama, we didn't even have a regular home yet. It took us awhile to find a church home, and until we did, "May the Lawd have mercy on our souls," would be prayed over us more than once. Judgment strained the air if we did not make it a priority to find a church home before finding a regular home. We needed a suitable answer to the looming church home question, or its members might threaten to send their church van to escort us to services. We left our address in the offering plate, so they knew where we lived.

Our first church visit was a bust. We missed the entire service, but not for lack of trying. We were all dressed up with nowhere to go, unable to locate the host church due to insufficient directions. On a 2.5 mile strip of Hughes Road, there were nine churches, four of which were at least a block wide. Hughes Road should've been called, "Church Street," but that street already existed, just one block over. Church Row would be more proper.

When my youngest daughter learned phonics, she sounded out the name of Hughes Road slowly, "H-h-u-u-g-gs...Hugs Road!" she would shout proudly. Church doors flung open to greet their guests as greeters shook hands and exchanged a lot of hugs. Therefore, Hughes Road, a.k.a. Hugs Road was an ideal location for Madison's churches. Three traffic policemen directed traffic on the quarter of a mile stretch every Sunday morning. Like a pretend Monopoly game, I imagined the traffic cop signaled directions and commanded, "Go to church, do not pass go, put $200 in the collection plate or you'll go directly to hell." Hughes Road was like a boardwalk with churches as large as hotels, but it was much like taking a "chance" card if you weren't familiar with all the church doctrines.

We missed church, but we didn't waste our 'Sunday best' church attire. We mingled with the church-goers in the lunch buffet lines at the local restaurants, so the day wasn't altogether lost. We learned that when a church service began was not nearly as important as to when it ended. The Sunday buffet had to be considered. Although we waited to be served, it gave us some satisfaction in knowing that at least we beat the Baptists to lunch. "The last shall be first," lesson didn't apply to the buffet line.

Nature continued to clash with religion when unpredictable tornadoes continued their destruction of churches. Tornadoes seemed to prey upon churches and weren't respecting the religious boundaries that we considered to be sacred places for the innocent: churches, hospitals, and schools. Whatever disturbed those sanctuaries struck a chord that cut deeply into our souls. It was hurtful, heart-wrenching, and it made us ask hard questions. A tornado touchdown in an open field was an act of God, but a tornado strike that assaulted the house of God…what could we call that?

A little before noon on Sunday, March 27, 1994, the Goshen United Methodist Church in Piedmont, AL held a crowded Palm Sunday service with the sweet voices of the children's choir serenading the sanctuary. Proud parents and grandparents enjoyed the symphony, certain that the Lord did too. The church was near capacity on one of the holiest days in the Christian faith. Suddenly in the midst of the chorus, the church roof collapsed on the innocent young as well as the devout old. Witnesses watched the church walls come to life, breathing in and out, before collapsing on the lives of fellow churchgoers. Nineteen church members were killed instantly, including the pastor's four-year old daughter. In what later became known as the Palm Sunday Tornado Outbreak, a powerful storm containing an F4 tornado slammed into the church and two other houses of worship that Sunday morning. In addition, eighty-six church members were injured, some carried out on the broken pews used as makeshift stretchers.

The town of Piedmont, the state of Alabama, as well as the nation mourned the losses and ranked it as the worst tornado event of the year. What initially blew apart the church actually brought it closer together. Churches around the country donated stained glass windows for a new building, church children were showered with Easter baskets, and citizens were compelled to give what they could, wanting to share their gifts during this tragedy.

According to Barbara Brown Taylor's "Tell Us a Resurrection Story," the pastor performed her daughter's funeral in the rubble. Church members wondered if Easter service would be celebrated that week. In answer to their questions, a big tent was erected on the church-less property and more than two hundred people attended the Easter sunrise service to hear the greatest story ever told. Gatherers were wrapped in white bandages and slings, and were a testimony to the Resurrection story of conquering death and the storms of life.

Following that incident, we learned that unless the church provided a basement for shelter, the church was no sanctuary against tornadoes. Those church steeples that sliced through the sky with pinnacles were seen slicing through telephone wires during the tornado aftermath. Such was the case at Fords Chapel, another United Methodist Church in Harvest, AL that was affected by a different tornado. It seemed that Methodist churches had a tornado bulls-eye on them. The two hundred-year old church was the oldest in the state, its sanctuary having being built in the 1800s. The congregation said goodbye to the ancient structure at approximately 4:25 p.m. on an April afternoon several years later. Mike Marshall with *The Huntsville Times* reported that a church clock found in the rubble was stamped with the time of the terror across its face. Hymnal pages were strewn across pastures and fields. Lines from the song, "Amazing Grace" were found in the mud.

The beloved hymn usually came to mind while in the throes of a tornado. It was a favorite among Alabama Christians while the winds raged. It was amazing grace that saved the lives of the children of Ford's Chapel. The Church's Mothers Morning Out program released the children before the tornado unleashed. The preschool classrooms had been destroyed, but fortunately the children had already gone home and there was no child left behind in the building. Only one church pew was intact. If you happened to be kneeling upon it during the whirlwind, you would've been saved by grace.

If a church was blown away, this was no excuse for missing Sunday services. Pastors and priests held their ground while believers came in droves to worship on the grounds that used to be the sanctuary. Sermons addressed the destruction and professed that God's kingdom was unshakable, a belief that resonated with members who could attest that nothing on this earth was immune to nature's wrath.

After violent storms, loving your neighbor takes on a deeper meaning. You did in fact, love your neighbor and were happy to see all of them, for a change. Church attendance soared in the days that followed the tempests. For those that lost their own home, a church home was a blessing. As long as tornadoes preyed, there would always be prayer.

12
ANDERSON HILLS

T minus sixteen years and counting. I blamed El Niño for the fact that 1995 was not a good year. El Niño, a misunderstood phenomenon, was a weather pattern responsible for warming or cooling ocean waters with trade winds. Supposedly this had something to do with the warmest Alabama winters on record during the mid-1990s. When something happened out of the ordinary, we blamed it on El Niño. If something was not right, it had come here from somewhere else, like fire ants or kudzu. In 1995, everything was El Niño's fault. He took the brunt of our dislikes and unexplained occurrences. I nearly died that February because of El Niño.

It was a fluke beautiful Saturday, smack in the middle of winter. I had been in Alabama long enough to know that there would be a penalty for a warm, temperate winter. But we took each unseasonable day as it came, never blaming the gorgeous weather on El Niño.

My second daughter came early and was still just a tiny newborn. Because she came into the world before her time, she was jaundiced. The temporary condition turned her skin a lovely olive tint which was very striking but apparently not healthy. Ultraviolet rays were the best cure for her jaundiced condition so the warm, February day was perfect for basking in the sunlight. I sifted through my winter sweaters, hunting for a pair of shorts to enjoy the fun in the sun. I grabbed a soft, baby quilt for the baby, hoping the sun's rays would lull her back to sleep. I felt as if I was cuddling a baby bat since she only slept by day.

With daughter in my arms, I swung open the storm door and burst out into the fresh, balmy air. I laid out the patchwork blanket and stretched out beside my baby on the grass. I soon jerked up and sat cross-legged, trying to find the ant that bit my exposed thigh. Those darn fire ants! El Niño must have brought them. I searched for the real culprit, but couldn't find the ant. My leg stung and the bite turned cherry red against my pale skin, glowing in the sun. I was suddenly very tired and needed a little nap. My little nap lasted five days and then I awoke in a delirium with a high fever of 104-105 degrees. I dreamed the strangest, recurring dream of traipsing through the wilderness and running from a tornado. I woke up sweating with my fever trying to break, but that didn't dispel the dreams.

After my Rocky Mountain-Spotted Fever diagnosis, I fainted at the doctor's office. It turned out that the little blood sucker was a tick that bit me, not a fire ant after all. El Niño probably caused the tick to reside in my residential backyard. After a long recovery from the illness, I finally got back on my feet again and eventually resumed teaching aerobics exercise classes in the middle of May. One May day, a student in my class had an exciting story to rehash. El Niño brought her something life threatening too.

She was mesmerized by the sky rushing overhead as she drove home on Jeff Road around 5:30 p.m. on May 18, 1995. The student witnessed a black funnel emerging from the sinister sky. The nervous sirens indicated that there was no mistaking the tornado. The massive twister appeared suddenly on her driver's side of the car. She knew she wasn't supposed to be in a vehicle during a tornado--one of the lessons learned from the 1989 twister that buried most of its victims in their cars. My friend panicked when her car door wouldn't budge. She was a prisoner in her own car. The pressure of the outer winds wouldn't allow her to escape. She dived across the front seat and managed to escape out of the passenger-side door instead. The funnel pummeled in the opposite direction and aimed towards the Anderson Hills subdivision. My friend watched all those houses that were next in line for the twister, while she lay shaking in the brush.

The tornado made contact with the ground in the late afternoon on May 18, 1995. It damaged 39 homes and destroyed 21 homes in the Anderson Hills subdivision, according to data from NOAA. Anderson Hills was a well-recognized community, lying on the corner of a major highway and surrounded like a fortress with a wall that rivaled the Great Wall of China. That wall was no match for the groundbreaking twister when it was toppled and its bricks were added to the rubble piles. Despite the destruction of the majority of the neighborhood, there were no fatalities in that area. Unfortunately, that same tornado took one life in the Oakdale Mobile Home Park before it took a direct path towards Anderson Hills. One man later died of injuries sustained by the funnels when his mobile home was destroyed. This F4 tornado packed a tremendous fury on its demolition course with twin tornadoes, double the trouble. Eyewitnesses confirmed at least two vortices within the main funnel.

Anderson Hills was not the origin of this tornado but it received the most news coverage based on its location and most obvious damage. The May 18, 1995 tornado was later labeled the first Anderson Hills tornado. Since this portion of the Tennessee Valley hosted so many intense tornadoes, it was necessary to name the funnels so that everyone knew which one was being discussed. It didn't help that the same areas had been hit by more than one tornado over the years. It didn't matter that they had been hit by more than one tornado in a single day. Unfortunately you couldn't even explain which tornado you meant when you stated, "the F4 tornado that hit Anderson Hills" because it wasn't precise enough.

The storms began to run together. But it was important to be on the same page when discussing Alabama tornadoes. We took all of them personally since the storms made it personal in their swath of demolition, striking some houses while skipping others. It helped to add descriptive adjectives when pinpointing the tornadoes. Phrases such as "Super Outbreak'" or "Day of Devastation" clarified the awesome but grueling power of nature and gave people an accurate picture when discussing past tornadoes.

The '95 tornado made its first touchdown outside of Limestone County near the city of Athens. There was no rain, just hail which resembled large white golf balls falling out of the sky. When the tornado formed, it was classified as an F0 based on wind speed. It later destroyed thirteen mobile homes in which one man later perished. This caused one to wonder why tornadoes always searched out the trailer parks or why mobile homes seemed to be on tornado paths.

It was documented that a cow passed away when a tree fell on it, cut down by the ferocious winds. Outsiders must understand our fetish with cows here in the Valley. We believed in sacred cows, or at least one of them. When Huntsville was first settled, a prominent citizen owned a prize cow named Lily Flagg. Lily Flagg received a first place ribbon at the county fair and national recognition, so her owner painted his mansion a buttery yellow in her honor. A party for the heifer was held for the wealthy with Lily Flagg shown to her audience on a raised platform built just for the occasion, and elevated to the position that she deserved. She was a true cash cow! The town of Huntsville embraced this cow with city streets, businesses and apartment complexes named for Lily Flagg. Over one hundred years later, I named my own daughter Elizabeth, "Lily" for short. We affectionately called her "Lily Flagg" sometimes.

The Anderson Hills tornado gathered intensity before it darted towards the subdivision. As it strengthened, the tornado crossed into Madison County with its exact point of entry at Harvest's Yarbrough Road. The tornado developed into F4 intensity and foreshadowed events years ahead of its time. Yarbrough Road's future was already set, so this F4 did not demolish the area yet. The 1995 tornado was on course for the Anderson Hills neighborhood, its namesake. But first it harassed Ford Chapel Road and the Methodist church there. It left the historical sanctuary intact, but future tornadoes would follow the same route and finish the job later. Nature's fury continued to careen out of control toward the Piggly Wiggly grocery store before Anderson Hills took a direct hit at 5:52 p.m.

The May 1995 tornado's reign of terror did not end in the neighborhood of Anderson Hills. It pressed on to Meridianville and the Buckhorn district. Folks complained about the title, Anderson Hills, since the tornado shattered lives outside of that community too. Looking back, it was an accurate name choice although it would later cause confusion over which Anderson Hills tornado you were discussing.

It was also in 1995 that Baron Services came into the picture. After the earlier Huntsville tornado in 1989, Bob Baron left his weather anchor position on TV and formed a company whose mission statement was built around the four concepts of weather: prediction, detection, dissemination and response. Baron Services would strive to streamline weather analysis and simplify it for the average viewer.

Baron's story is similar to Benjamin Franklin's. Franklin used lightning to discover electricity and Baron used lightning to discover the science behind developing tornadoes. The lightning was the key in both cases. For a time, Baron worked as a meteorologist in Tampa, Florida. While there, he used specialized equipment to detect lightning. If a device could detect lightning feed, the tool could also detect the most active part of a thunderstorm, Baron concluded. He moved back to Huntsville and formed a 'Mom and Pop shop' with his wife as the bookkeeper and his son as the salesman. Baron Services started in Bob Baron's home. His house was outfitted like a TV station.

Baron received a NASA grant for his Storm Tracker, which he developed from the lightning tracker concept. His weather tool would hook onto live radar to do the mapping. Later it would have zooming capabilities to detect the direction and wind speed of the storm, coupled with the latitudes and longitudes of the communities that the storm would likely affect. The device made a box on the screen with the storm's estimated arrival time at each destination. Not only did Baron Services analyze the storm data, but also added a forecasting component to indicate whether the storms would intensify. At first Baron used refurbished Doppler radar equipment that was about to be discarded. In 1995, Baron Services built its own radars and relocated to Research Park in Huntsville.

I later had the opportunity to tour the facility and was impressed to see the operations room with several large screens mounted on the wall, monitoring weather from different parts of the world. Baron Services had clients in Romania and Southeast Asia, in addition to those in the United States. At the time of my tour, only four people were working the consoles, but during severe weather, all stations were manned.

Mr. Baron also showed me a seam in the hallway which separated the operations center from the business center. In case of violent weather, the operations center was built to withstand anything, he told me. The rest of the building could be destroyed at the seams, but the operations bunker would survive. He described it as a suspended box inside of a box. When I asked him about his own tornado bunker at home, he replied, "I take shelter just like everyone else. I have a little closet under the stairs."

13

LABOR DAY TORNADO

T minus thirteen years and counting. My personal Labor Day came in April. The rest of the nation celebrated the holiday in September, but my third child was scheduled to be induced April 16th, 1998, so it was my 'Labor Day.' I felt apprehensive in scheduling my own baby's actual birthdate. There was so much to worry about, look forward to, and plan. When a mother is ready to give birth to her child, the most pressing thing on her mind is not the weather, so the forecast was ignored that day.

The weather was not important when I gave birth to my first two girls. My first child pushed her way into the world, and while my husband pushed with both of us, he developed a nosebleed and the delivery nurses had to turn their attention to him. My second child came even quicker. I paced like a caged lion in the crowded emergency room, but we had to wait like everyone else. As labor pains escalated, I leaned against the wall of the E.R. and felt a puddle pooling around me—oh no, not again, I thought. But it was my water that broke. I had worried needlessly about having a baby in an elevator. Never did I imagine that I would have a baby while on display for all, leaning against the emergency room wall! Lucky for all, it was only a close call.

My third child was induced in a plush, newly remodeled hospital room with a television. A first time for everything, I was in charge of the remote control. No longer did I need to pretend that the nurse's finger was a birthday candle in which to blow out. I had a TV mounted in front of my face and it became my new focal point. I labored while watching the news of a tornado ripping through Nashville, TN. The footage showed the tornado clipping Nashville's new downtown stadium.

The doctor administered an epidural anesthesia, so I couldn't feel a thing. The staff interrupted my television programming to tell me that it was time to push. It was not as dramatic as having a baby in an elevator or a waterfall down the wall, but the drama would come later. Just as I gave the final push, a warning bleep went across the screen. Doctors glanced at my monitors, but it was a weather alert on the TV. Another tornado launched into Fayetteville, TN just across the state border. It was coming. And so was she!

My baby girl was born at 3:23 p.m., the same time the tornado touched down in Alabama. My husband held the baby, kissed us both 'goodbye,' and then sped home to our other children who were in my mother's care. I was at the other end of town, numb from the waist down, in the birthing wing of Huntsville Hospital.

The nurses whisked me into a wheel chair. I saw my legs flopping, but couldn't feel them. I hoped the flailing limbs weren't going to be an issue. They placed my nine pound infant in my arms and wheeled me to the lobby with the other patients. This baby born in the midst of drama was the same baby we called Lily or "Lily Flagg" affectionately. After all, she weighed over nine pounds, as much as a baby calf. Some mothers still labored in the hallway, so I swallowed my complaints. There was always someone worse off than myself. All patients were moved to the interior halls, away from windows and flying surgical instruments. Those of us still attached to IV stands were holding our finished products, cheering the laboring mothers to victory from our galley of wheelchairs.

The tornado continued to blow past Alabama A & M College and we were next in line. A different alarm squealed next to me and I almost dropped my baby. It was just a new father carrying his newborn into the stairwell, seeking shelter. No one bothered to match his ID bracelet with the baby's. Then, there was silence—the eerie kind of silence.

In an instant the threat was gone. Huntsville dodged the bullet again. My only safety plan was to cradle my baby with my head bowed low to protect her. I was already bowing my head in thanksgiving that the tornado bypassed the hospital. Years later, I would watch a televised tornado that terrorized a hospital in Joplin, Missouri. I could still taste my own feeling of helplessness in a life-threatening situation.

I looked at my new daughter swaddled in my arms, and I knew that she would be a drama queen of near misses. Had she asked if the stork brought her, I could tell her that the stork was travelling at a high rate of speed being followed by a tornado. I made a mental note not to have another baby during tornado season. In Alabama, that would mean that half of the year was not a good time to be fertile.

Shelly Van Meter Miller

TIMELINE TO TRAGEDY

14
TWISTED

T minus 15 months and counting. Some twisters demanded more attention than others, but we shouldn't skip the weaker tornadoes since they didn't skip us. The first ten years of the Millennium were quiet ones for Huntsville, weather-wise. This was not the case for the entire state of Alabama. Somehow the November 24, 2001 tornado blitz missed our town. With a record 36 tornado touchdowns in our state, this was the worst tornado outbreak since 1974. Miraculously, Huntsville was spared in the deluge. But the clock was ticking and our countdown began when various twisters struck our town beginning in 2010. These twisters were the stepping stones to the worst tornado outbreak in Alabama history. January of 2010 began the countdown to touchdown.

The University of Alabama football team counted its touchdowns and won its thirteenth national championship. Alabama sports fans went crazy over the victory and their highly revered Coach "S". Some even suggested that he run for president and lead the country as he led his winning team. With the championship won, fans earned the right to party until the Super Bowl, but many bizarre occurrences stole the show from the win.

For starters, a 7.0 magnitude earthquake devastated the country of Haiti, killing 300,000 Haitians. The Deepwater Horizon oil well exploded in the Gulf of Mexico, killing its crew and gushing thousands of gallons of oil daily into Alabama's coastal waters. Chilean miners would spend sixty-eight days in the belly of the earth, trapped inside a collapsed mine before they were rescued. In addition, the Tiger Woods sex scandal, Apple introducing the iPad to the world, and a UFO sighting in Manhattan stole the world's attention. All the bad news completely eclipsed the tornado that hit Huntsville in January. Understandably, an isolated tornado paled in comparison to the world's ongoing catastrophes that year.

Perhaps those of us in Alabama should have paid more attention to the January 21st twister. No loss of life resulted from the EF2 tornado so we thought no more about it. But an out-of-season tornado striking North Alabama in January meant that we were vulnerable to a tornado attack any time of the year, not just during our two tornado seasons, spring and fall. Instead, tornadoes could strike anytime and anywhere, shifting the game rules. Twisted weather became the norm.

Recently, my daughter showed me a picture of a tornado looming over the city of Huntsville. The picture appeared to be a fake one with a perfectly formed tornado centered over the church with the egg-beater Jesus mural. I assumed that someone photo-shopped the tornado over the town but my daughter declared that it was indeed a real picture taken on January of 2010. I had completely forgotten about the January tornado, and I even knew of friends with property damage from that particular storm. "People might get mad if you forget their tornado, Mom," my daughter stated. She was right. We were possessive of our tornadoes. When they affected us, they became our own personal tornadoes. If we could have disowned them, we would have gladly done so.

The picture of the tornado jarred my memory. The way I remember that January afternoon, my same daughter called me from the kitchen, "Mom, look at the sky. Isn't it pretty?" The black cloud merged with the sunset and formed an abnormal jade shade that rolled over the rooftops across the street.

"No, it's not pretty," I replied. Too many times I had seen a cloud of darkness disguised as an Angel of Light. In most places, a green color meant 'go,' but in Alabama, green meant tornado. Within seconds, the weather tower revved its siren and the neighborhood stepped outdoors to watch the wall cloud pass.

The tornado began near the Space and Rocket Center which is located on I-565. The twister avoided the Saturn rocket and touched down on Redstone Arsenal's Goss Road and then tormented

Huntsville's historic Old Town and Five Points area, damaging homes and leaving three people injured. Although the twister caught us off guard in January, it was one of the most filmed touchdowns because the tornado was so obvious and deliberate. The tornado spawned right before our eyes, and in the middle of a beautiful sunset. As a result, the twister didn't appear sinister but instead resembled a giant pink puff of cotton candy flavoring the sky as it drifted by. But this beautiful cloud was a wolf in sheep's clothing. Many onlookers declared, "Isn't it pretty?" until the pastel funnel dropped and twisted with muddy debris. Moments later, the twilight twister was just another ugly black funnel shrouded in lightning. It wreaked its usual havoc on downtown Huntsville with winds packing 150 mph, strong enough to slam a truck into someone's home. Trees twisted and snapped like chopsticks. The innocent looking tornado left a muddy mess.

We wanted to believe that the January tornado was a freak of nature along with 2010's other unnatural events. It would not be the last time that a tornado struck Alabama in the month of January though. One much more lethal storm would haunt Birmingham in a different January in the future. The weather seemed to twist more and more with each passing year.

Shelly Van Meter Miller

15
WHITEOUT

T minus three months and counting. January of 2011 began with a beautiful white surprise. Snow! Helpless, I could only watch as my husband careened out of control, cartwheeling past me to land in a heap at the bottom of the hill. I squinted through the glare to detect movement but I, too, was paralyzed. I glanced down and saw that the lower half of my body was missing, buried knee-deep in the avalanche. I hoisted one leg at a time from the snowdrift and barreled downhill toward my husband. He chose a snowboard with handlebars as the descent ride of choice down Dublin Park's snow covered hill. Now he would pay the price.

Face planted in the snow, he came up for air with bushy eyebrows and a fuzzy mustache caked in white. The snow mustache prompted my joke, "Got snow?" I shook with laughter at my own pun, nearly bursting my sides. It really did burst my bladder as I felt a warm sensation down my legs. Then the joke was on me. My children were well into their teens, but they weren't familiar with yellow snow yet.

For nearly two decades, the closest thing that resembled a snow covering was when the cotton turned white after the defoliant was sprayed or when the Bradford Pear blossoms carpeted the ground in the spring. Snow seemed to halt at the Tennessee state line and did not drift one inch across the border. I have pitiful pictures of my children sliding down a small mound of frost in a recycling bin. And we called that a snow day. The last real snow day caused the blizzard of March 1993. The fluke whiteout in the middle of spring left our cityscape blackened. The cold snapped the trees and zapped the blossoms with charred buds. An early April snow shower did not bring May flowers. However it brought more babies than the stork. Huntsville had a city-wide baby boom of children born exactly nine months after the blizzard. The town shut down but the weather closings didn't interfere with all the socializing. Evidently couples found ways to pass the time during the inclement weather.

This January 2011 scenery wasn't quite the same Norman Rockwell backdrop with a sledding accident and yellow snow, but the season's snowscape that fell on Christmas morning the week before was indescribable. I opened the curtains, even threw open the sash as the sun beamed off the pearly snow-covered ground. The powder glittered and danced in the light, throwing diamond prisms throughout the room. I felt like I was inside my very own snow globe. The snow in the tall pines puffed like baby powder in the slight breeze. The cardinals were beside themselves, eagerly hopping from branch to branch. Their crimson breasts contrasted with the glowing snow and sapphire sky was a picture worth a million words.

Out of the neighbor's woods, a red fox trotted past, kicking up snow as it scampered. I was mesmerized by the dreamy storybook scene of beauty orchestrated with snowfall made to glisten, even cueing the sun to shine brightly, and finally coordinating the fox on the run. My curious cat was also entranced by the wonderland and climbed the windowsill to share my view. Kitty pawed at the errant snowflakes that drifted slowly to the porcelain ground. Both of us gazed out the window at the neighbor's Christmas light display still lit from Christmas Eve. The animated deer bobbed its head and twinkled in the early morning light.

I couldn't decide whether to wake my children to wish them a Merry Christmas, displaying the snow as if the gift of it was my idea, or to slip outside and be the first to experience that first, crunchy snow step and wake the kids with a snowball pounding their window. I savored the moment, pouring myself a warm mug of cider with cinnamon and whipped cream spiraled on top, while my breakfast casserole preheated in the oven. Mornings just didn't get any better than this.

The upstairs would soon creak with the padding of slippers that skipped the steps two at a time. Gift wrap would rip as boxes were plundered to the background tune of Lee Greenwood crooning, "Let it snow, let it snow, let it snow." Then someone would yell, "Timber!" as the Christmas tree snapped against the hardwood floor. The girls stripped the tree's boughs in their search for the hidden green pickle ornament, its finder snatching an extra present. Santa bought a new tree stand after one too many pickle search and rescues.

An Alabama white Christmas was a dream come true, a check on my bucket list. Nothing surpassed its splendor except maybe the silent Christmas night just after twilight when the snow muffled the sounds of my quiet walk around the neighborhood. Window drapes were drawn but I could peer between the folds to see family-filled dens with a fire in the hearth. Like watching pretty fish glide in an aquarium, calmness filled me. The warmth emanated within the walls as the chimney smoke curled into the crisp, evening air. It felt like there really was peace on earth.

The snow day turned into a snow week and we rang in 2011 with nine inches of snow on the ground. I never imagined that I would have to sweep snow from the palm tree fronds. With only a couple of road plows for the entire town, streets and parking lots were ice rinks. Both work and school were on indefinite sabbaticals, closed for business. The hill at the local high school was the best sledding in Madison. Inner tubes, clothes baskets, cardboard, and even air mattresses cascaded down the snowy banks. The snow moguls popped holes in three of our pool floats, but the thrill ride was worth it. Kids soared through the air as if on flying saucers, a modern version of the Jetsons. Alabama made the most of the snowfall; not a flake was wasted. But just as in The Year without a Santa Claus, we should have known that Mr. Heat Miser and Cold Miser cut a deal for January's blustery snow show in our Southern town of Southtown. We had no idea what price would be exacted for each one of those snowflakes. Never one to look a gift horse in the mouth, we thought the winter extravaganza was "snow" much fun. Three swim floats-around $30. Snow in Alabama? We would figure the cost later. Husband face planted in the snow-priceless!

It was a beautiful month cloaked in snow, but to our dismay, it was the first weather fluke on 2011's timeline to tragedy. Forecasters could have rightfully predicted more extreme weather to come. We shouldn't have been surprised if they said, "The weather will be cloudy these next few months with a chance of tornado flurries."

Shelly Van Meter Miller

16
THE MURDERS OF MADISON COUNTY

T minus two months and counting. February made us shiver. It was another dismal February Friday when my daughter dressed for school. "Can you drop me off at the path, Mom?" I guessed I could, but it was such a pain. Her middle school was only three blocks away but I didn't think that even I could carry her heavy backpack for three steps. The foggy morning dropped a curtain of crusty ice over my windshield. The icy windows wouldn't have caused me such grief if I owned a bona fide ice scraper. I was forced to use the edges of an outdated cassette case from the last century as my scraper.

I whisked my daughter to the path that led to the school and practically kicked her out of the car, not to be mean, but for momentum to propel her and her massive book bag forward. I forgot and had to chase her down to pray with her. I never let a school day start without praying over my children. Usually rushed, I at least managed to pray, "Lord, keep her safe and healthy today," which translated to: "I'll call you back later when I have time, God" kind of prayer. Had I known what the day had in store for my daughter, I would've held her prisoner in the car against her will and never let her go to school that morning. Every other middle school mom would have done the same thing had they known what the future held. The empty school hallways would have echoed in silence instead of ached in agony.

"Hey," my daughter greeted her schoolmate. "Hey," he replied.

The hurried greeting was all students managed to utter in the hallways between classes. The class bell signaled a mass exodus of students flooding the halls, anxious to see and to be seen. A maze of backpacks dodged and zigzagged to the book lockers like salmon swimming upstream. Pranksters slammed their books on the floor for a knee-jerk reaction and locker doors slammed for effect with loud smacks. When a single gunshot rang through the halls, most students didn't even flinch.

When the students realized what happened, some hid behind poles, some under tables, and some fled the building. All but two students ran for cover. Of the two, one still held the smoking gun, and the other lay lifeless in a pool of blood. Like a chain reaction, pandemonium permeated the hall as panicked teens scrambled for sanctuary. Teachers shoved students inside classrooms while wrestling their backpacks to the floors. Classroom doors that once flung open for students eager to escape were slammed shut by school children seeking shelter. It was unreal. It was surreal. It was a Code Red and it was allegedly cold-blooded murder.

My neighbor brought the bad news to my front door. I was confused as to why she stood on my porch with her hair dripping wet in the middle of winter. Suddenly, my stomach dropped to the ground as her words sank into my skull. I deciphered my neighbor's muddled message: There was a shooting at the middle school and my daughter was trapped inside the school with a gunman!

"Please be okay, please be okay!" I agonized. My ears were ringing as they did right before I was about to faint. Then my cell phone rang while in my hands which startled me more. It was my husband informing me that our daughter had texted him she was "okay," one of the quickest answers to prayer I had ever had. Relief flooded my veins, along with a gush of guilt when I realized that one middle school mom would not receive the same text but instead would be overcome with grief.

My reunion with my daughter was bittersweet. No words could explain my gratitude, but I could only hold her as she shook with sorrow. Her friend was dead. Only an hour earlier, they had spoken to each other before he walked to his death at the other end of the hall, allegedly killed by his own classmate. "Hey," was the last word my daughter shared with the deceased. From that day forward, I made a vow to learn to text so that I could communicate with loved ones during emergencies. I soon mastered texting and sent texts to all family members. My first text to my daughter was, "Hey."

As we exited her fallen classmate's funeral, a separate 911 call was placed that same afternoon, pulling the police escorts from one tragic scene to another. On the campus of the University of Alabama in Huntsville, another school shooting occurred. However, the hand that pulled the trigger was not that of a student, but presumably of a biology professor. The professor was charged in the shooting deaths of her colleagues, leaving three dead and three seriously wounded. The suspected motive of denied tenure had allegedly fueled her rage and according to police reports, she fired bullets repeatedly into fellow faculty members during a staff meeting. Police cuffed the professor and escorted her to a squad car while EMTs removed the lifeless bodies of the victims on stretchers.

One February later in 2011, Huntsville still reeled from aftershocks of the murders in Madison County. Children feared attending school and parents feared sending them. The town had been rocked, and peace of mind ambushed. The year began on shaky ground as we sought to recover before another ground-shaking event rattled us. We forged through February's forsaken weather, anxious to escape the haunting memories. We looked forward to spring's promise of new life as we gladly marched into March.

Shelly Van Meter Miller

17
DAY OF DEVASTATION

T minus 1 month and counting. March was a blur. We said things like, "I can't believe it's March already," the same thing we said every year. Spring break came and went and the high school prom came before we were ready. The school year would be downhill from there. Nothing out of the ordinary happened in March. Then came the April showers. We were showered alright, but not with gentle spring rains.

We called it the Day of Devastation. Those were the words attempting to describe the desolation and death that descended on Alabama on one dreadful day. April 27, 2011, was a day like no other. It was the worst weather disaster in our state, and for many, it was the worst day of their lives.

The entire nation was bombarded by tornadoes that day, but Alabama took the brunt of the storms. By all estimations, it was two years' worth of tornadoes in twenty-four hours. Out of the record 62 confirmed twisters that pulverized our red clay, two of them were EF5 tornadoes, the fiercest of the storms on the Fujita scale. Another violent EF4 tornado touched down in "T-town," Tuscaloosa, and terrorized many Huntsville students who attended college there at the University of Alabama. Parents of the Huntsville students suspended their worries temporarily in order to run for cover while tornadoes tormented our own town simultaneously. The tornadoes came at us from all directions. NOAA called it the "greatest swarm of tornadoes." Much like the stars falling in 1833, the sky was falling on

Alabama with sonic booms of destruction.

The tornadoes came in waves. The twisters that demolished Huntsville's outlying counties were considered the third wave of the day. The National Weather Service labeled the multi-vortex tornado that persecuted Tuscaloosa as number #44, coming between #43 that hit the town of Harvest, just outside of Huntsville and tornado #45 which carved a trail of terror through East Limestone, another surrounding county. Alabama's tornado assault was relentless, thorough, and fatal. America lost 327 of its citizens in one day of storms, including 243 in Alabama. It was not a good day to be an Alabamian.

The deadliest twister of the day, as well as in all of Alabama's history, was the #37 Hackleburg tornado. The EF5 wrought destruction in three states and scarred the ground for ninety miles. Jeff Hansen, in his *Birmingham News* article, "April Tornadoes Legacy," reported that scientists captured the storm on a high tech imaging device and later reviewed its formation, describing it as "…a high dome of rain just in front of a tornadogenic thunderstorm, held aloft by gale-force winds shooting thousands of feet straight up into the air." The Hackleburg tornado formed in the thermal boundary, where cooler air met moist warm air. This fed the ferocity of the killer tornado. When scientists viewed the storm data, they gasped. They knew what it meant for a tornado to form in the thermal boundary. It was compared to the place where waves break in the ocean, a place of intense focused energy and power. For the town of Hackleburg, this meant decimation. Seventy-two lives would be claimed. No other town experienced more destruction than Hackleburg, where even the pavement was sucked up as if the ground was being unzipped.

The Hackleburg storm was the parent storm of Huntsville's twisters, 132 miles away from their genesis. The supercell began in Mississippi, entered Alabama, and cut through six counties, before exiting into Tennessee. The description of the Hackleburg tornado did not do it justice. There were no words to describe the devastation. Huntsville's Madison County was dealt five days of darkness from the Hackleburg supercell which originated over one hundred miles away. It was a monster of a storm.

The second deadliest storm of the day, and in our state history, was the EF4 tornado that reduced Tuscaloosa to rubble. Although another powerful EF5 storm hit Rainsville, AL on April 27th, making two EF5 tornadoes to touch down in our state that day, the #44 Tuscaloosa tornado took more lives, killing 53 victims. The situation was so dire that the Weather Channel's Jim Cantore tweeted: "Pray for Tuscaloosa." The outcome was dreadful, as he expected. The fatalities occurred during "dead week," the week before students' final exams. Because of the fatalities and seven miles of destruction, the university closed, cancelling the rest of the school year. Final exams never happened. Graduation was delayed until August of 2011. Of the six Alabama students who died in the storms, some were expected to graduate on stage in the following weeks, but their lives were taken before their diplomas were delivered into their hands.

Alabama held the highest tornado death rate and that was before April 27, 2011. In one day, hundreds more fatalities were added to the grim statistics, securing Alabama's ranking for tornado deaths in the nation. Data gathered from the Tornado Recovery Action Council of Alabama recently announced the staggering statistics. Out of the 67 counties in Alabama, 35 of them suffered tornado damage on April 27th. The tornado's swath of destruction measured 1,206 miles long through our state. Nearly 23,000 homes and businesses were damaged or destroyed on the same day, incurring close to $5.5 billion in cost. In the city of Tuscaloosa, within six minutes 7000 people became unemployed. But the numbers did not tell the whole story. Each number was somebody's job. Each number was somebody's money. Each number was somebody's house. In the end, each number was somebody's life.

We knew the storms were coming. We took shelter from those storms, but our shelters and interior rooms were no match for a ruthless EF5 tornado. One storm victim lost his home when it exploded under the tornado's wrath. The owner was an icon in Huntsville's weather arena for years. As a meteorologist, he knew what to expect and directed others to safety in his nearby tornado shelter. He was still injured during the storm. Tornadoes do not play favorites.

Of the victims that perished that day, at least ten of them sought shelter in a basement underground. Some victims died while on their way to a shelter. Heart attacks accounted for some of those deaths. One person died without a scratch, but had suffered a broken neck.

Others died while protecting their families. Grandparents lay across grandchildren to shelter them from the coming tornado. The children would survive because of their sacrifice. The tornadoes took one twin and left the other behind. Pregnant mothers went into premature labor and those lives were counted among the lost as well. One child lost his parents, his brother, and his leg. No, numbers did not even begin to tell it all.

It would forever be called the Day of Devastation because we were devastated, for lack of any other word to describe the chaos. The financial costs could be calculated over time, but the real costs could never be measured. The storms that passed would not fade quickly into our pasts because of the intangible costs: the cost of children tormented with panic attacks on cloudy days, the cost of adults wearing a mouthpiece at night to keep from screaming in their recurring nightmares, and the cost of loved ones absent during the next holiday. All the while, the limbless trees, tar paper tattered roofs, and weedy wastelands were a constant reminder of our losses.

Looking back to that fateful day, we would have done a lot of things differently. Even the smallest change could have changed the course of someone's life. While one friend survived in a closet, his other friends died in the hallway on the other side of the wall. The slightest move could have saved their lives. As much as we rehashed that Wednesday, it never brought anyone back. Alabama was targeted and marked that day. The countdown was over. T minus 0. Ground Zero.

18
NIGHT AT THE E.R.

Bedtime was a nightly ritual when our children were young. It was an hour long ceremony ousting the children out of our bed and tucking them into their own beds. Now our girls had cell phones that tucked them into bed every evening. They texted: "Goodnight," and then "twittered" the night away. The last time I tucked my girls in was tornado night. I thanked God for my family as I hugged my husband and each child tightly. One deadly storm already passed through but we weren't convinced that the tornadoes were finished with us. Nighttime came quicker than usual without street light reminders. Power outages across the Valley left citizens without television, cell phones, or internet connections. Except for the sound of the emergency sirens, it would have been a silent night. Instead it was a chaotic tornado night.

I released the whereabouts of my secret candle stash that I horded, still in their cellophane wraps. To me, the candle was ruined if the wick was charred. On this tornado night, candles graced every room of our house, which made me paranoid of a fire from the open candle flames. Without smoke detectors and a way to call the fire department, I regarded the unattended flames as another disaster waiting to happen. People across the state of Alabama were doing the same thing we were doing that night. One death actually did occur from a fire on 'tornado night.' As a precaution, I slept downstairs to monitor the candles on the first floor.

Before making my bed on the couch, I inspected the locked doors and glanced into the black onyx night. I saw silhouettes of the other houses on our cul-de-sac, and knew their placement in the blackness because flashlights circled throughout. It appeared as if burglars were in every home. In reality, my neighbors were unsure of their own footsteps in the shadows. The roving flashlights reminded me of hunting ghost crabs on the beach. Instead of the sounds of the surf to lull us to sleep, waves of ambulance sirens pierced the night.

I watched the candle's flickering light reflect off the mirror and dance on the fireplace wall. It reminded me of the nuns' convent and a different tornado warning when I was young. Like before, I remained untouched, but knew that others were likely to be in the path of destruction. Sooner or later I would know the truth. I willed myself to sleep and postponed the painful thoughts. My emotions were drained and only sleep could refill the quarry. I threw my covers off one last time to locate a can of wasp spray to place on the ottoman next to me. In case an intruder chose to disturb our slumber, a jet stream of wasp spray would spurt in his eyes. I even unscrewed the spray cap, ready to 'wasp' anything that moved or went 'bump' in the night. With my hand near the trigger, exhaustion took over and sleep finally came.

Because I was overtired, it took a second for me to realize what happened next. A shadow crawled on hands and knees toward the couch on which I slept. Flustered and panicked, I sat up and scrambled for that wasp spray. My heart skipped more than one beat before I recognized my husband's voice calling out to me and him reaching for my hands. I kept asking, "What are you saying? What? What?" Between his incoherent moans and my heart pumping wildly, I couldn't hear. I finally deciphered two words: kidney and stone.

Oh no, it couldn't be! I knew what kidney stone meant. It meant hospital. It meant emergency. It meant drugged up. It meant pain and suffering and a miserable wait in the emergency waiting room. My husband had a knack for crashing parties by forming kidney stones during major holidays or events. There were Thanksgiving, Christmas Day, and Halloween kidney stone stories. Tornado Night would be added to the ongoing list. Hopefully the stone was small enough to pass. If not, emergency surgery was needed. Men likened passing a kidney stone to having a baby. Unless the stone weighed nine pounds and left stretch marks, I disagreed. But I had never passed a kidney stone, so I wouldn't know.

The battery-powered mantle clock revealed that it was after midnight. We planned to traipse through the night to the one place that no one wanted to be, and on possibly the worst night ever for the emergency room. It was no place for our girls to spend Tornado Night. Our teens climbed into one bed, thinking that there was safety in numbers. I kissed their cuddled figures goodbye and drove my husband into the haunted night.

Without traffic lights or other cars on the road, we only had to worry about staying on the road while making it to the hospital in time to deliver the kidney stone. The sound of tires crunching gravel hinted that we weren't on the roadway. I wished they had finished building the new Madison Hospital on this tornado night. Huntsville Hospital was still a hop, skip, and what seemed like a plane ride away. A flash of bright lights flooded our car. A policeman laid in wait for curfew breakers, but he either recognized our hazard lights or haggard looking faces in the spotlight.

Speeding along on Interstate I-565, I could have stopped the car in the middle of the Interstate and run a Chinese fire drill, for there was no sign of activity. My heart skipped several beats when I thought that I had missed an exit and was lost. Nothing looked familiar in the blackness. Everything looked dead. Finally some recognizable landmarks appeared above the overpass. Two buildings illuminated the land like a runway with Monte Sano Mountain looming in the distance. The only two structures with generated light were the jail and the hospital. I drove into the light toward the hospital. Once there, it felt more like the jail and we were its inmates doing time.

I drove into the congested parking garage, tempted to park in the handicapped spot. Anyone ill enough to visit the emergency room was handicapped in some way. I scanned the waiting room for open seats, but there weren't any. People lined the walls. My husband's pain caused him to pace like a caged lion, so he wouldn't sit even if there was an open chair. I leaned against the wall of the waiting room and déjà vu reminded me of the last time when my water broke on the same wall. I shuddered at the thought and joined my husband in pacing.

I couldn't help but overhear painful conversations around me. One lady was desperate to locate a loved one having followed the ambulance that carried him. The staff was unable to find him in their system. A suited employee dressed like an undertaker stooped in front of the distraught woman and asked her whether her loved one was alive before the ambulance ride and was it possible that the victim did not arrive alive. The representative then indicated that they would check the morgue. What an agonizing solution.

My husband shuffled along, carrying his bedpan for nausea. The triage nurse called his name and we left the waiting room filled with loss and heartache to enter a hall of pain and suffering. The hallway was overly crowded with tornado victims and their families. We begged for pardon as we parted through the crowd to get to our reserved emergency room. I stared at the bedpan and understood the reason for our accelerated health service. A bedpan implied a sense of urgency, but it had not been our intention to exploit the bedpan plan.

While awaiting treatment, patients practiced patience that they didn't normally have. Everyone extended grace to one another that night in our disaster-ridden town. Doctors and nurses did their best while we prayed that their best was good enough, so we didn't get upset when someone stole the bed out of our hospital room. Maybe it was needed for one of the emergency surgeries. I knew of one victim admitted to the hospital that evening, undergoing one of eight surgeries within two weeks to save her severed leg. Two chairs were left in the room so we didn't have to sit on the floor. It was a horrible place to spend the night. Surrounded by gloom and doom, I wondered how our city could recover. We often wondered that about Huntsville.

This was one night in which my husband would not have said no to drugs. Ironically, we received a prescription for pain medication that we tossed in the back seat of the car since the entire city was without power and no pharmacies would open anytime soon. The hospital was alive with generator power, but the rest of the city fended for itself. We were anxious to get home to our children, to love them, hug them tightly, and rest for what lay ahead in the uneasy days to come. I prayed for my babies, my husband's health, the lady searching for her loved one, those suffering in the hall, whoever stole our hospital bed, and for all the tornado victims that I didn't know about yet.

AFTERMATH

19
THE SOCIAL NETWORK

Tornado terror. Total blackout. Emergency room. In one night we encountered all three traumas. The next morning we were too tired to pick up the pieces. We had every right to sleep late, but sleep wouldn't come for the sole reason that we needed sleep. After a nervous night of pitch blackness and relentless emergency sirens, it was not suitable to curse the morning sun for shining through the blinds or to reprimand the birds cooing their pleasant wake-up calls. We only had one pressing item on the agenda that we knew of…passing a kidney stone. 'We' because it was a two person job with one to pass the stone and the other person to encourage (nag) the passer.

One by one, family members drifted downstairs and stared at one another. "What are we going to eat?" "What are we going to do?" The children were nervous as if the impromptu family gathering was part of a plot from the *Hansel and Gretel* story whereby we would take them into the forest and leave them there. We were still without power, but it wasn't the end of the world. Well, maybe. For our kids, it was technically the end of their iWorld with no electronic devices to rule over them.

The last time that adults felt so helpless was on the eve of Y2K when computers were supposed to take over the world. We imagined that nuclear warheads would launch themselves and that information would rewrite history, deleting all traces that man ever existed. The only way we coped with that possible dire outcome was to horde gallons of distilled water and store lime Jell-O. But the end never came when the clock struck midnight on the year 2000 and we didn't turn into pumpkins. It took ten years to empty the water gallons. During the current power outage, we wished we had that water, but not so much the Jell-O.

On April 28, 2011, we were faced with the same dilemma. We were again at the mercy of technology, except with even more to lose. We would have to co-exist in the real world instead of a virtual one. For some, it was unknown territory, like goldfish out of the aquarium gasping without their technical gills. For another few, technology left us behind after Al Gore claimed to have invented the internet, and we were delighted to depart from the computer-dominated lifestyle. We were excited to take the day and do something we wanted to do for a long, long time…nothing.

That next day was fresh with the slate wiped clean. Nature fled the scene of the crime that it had committed and attempted to erase all signs of wrongdoing. It was hard to believe that the day's baby blue skies were brought to us by the previous day's tornado marathon. The day after the storm was a breath of fresh air and smelled as fresh as pine. So crisp was the pine scent that it reminded me of Christmas although it was April. While we did nothing that day, nearby neighbors were removing massive pine trees from their bedrooms. An EF0 tornado had struck only two blocks away and uprooted countless trees. The pine smell was extra pungent for them as they picked up the pieces of their lives, scattered by a wind that spun out of control, but stopped spinning just short of our neighborhood. We continued to do nothing and were oblivious to what others around us were going through. We had no idea what went on outside of our back door. We were powerless, phoneless, and textless.

As we basked in our lounge chairs, our three teens lined up in front of us and parroted the two words that drive parents crazy: "We're bored." If I ever mouthed those words to my parents, I found myself dusting the top of the refrigerator or some other useless task. "We want to go somewhere," they complained. Our cars didn't have enough gas for joyriding and besides, everything was closed with the power outage. The lack of Facebook was starting to get to our children and they didn't 'like' not having a button to push for instant friends. Cell phone towers were also disabled. I poked fun at my children as they circled our home to position themselves in the best alignment with the city's closest cell phone tower in the hopes of reception. They had a look of desperation on their faces, the same look as when I grounded them from their phone or laptop.

I had a brilliant idea and presented it to the kids. "Why don't you find your friends and talk to them face-to-face?" I suggested. It was as if a solar light came on for the kids. They dragged out the ten speed bikes and even a Razor scooter from the back of the garage. The tires were flatter than my Volvo's tires but the girls learned new skills in order to use the wheels. We watched as they clumsily operated a bicycle pump like 'The Three Stooges' and doubled over from laughter. The bike helmets were still in the tornado shelter, but they were one short, so our oldest daughter did without. As it so happened, riding a bicycle without a helmet was on her bucket list of things to do. Next she would want to run with scissors!

The Huntsville's Angels (my girls) biked around the neighborhood and returned only when their stomachs growled. They also brought with them an extra ten mouths to feed, including teenage boys who were hungry from pushing pedals all day. I found myself hiding the bread and stashing food supplies in foreign places. If teenage boys' appetites were anything like teenage girls, we would soon be standing in the food line.

I watched the group of bikers walk bow-legged into our house. They liberally discussed their newfound blisters on their bottoms due to the bicycle seats. Teenagers were used to texting their life stories and didn't hold anything back during the dinner table discussion. The social network was changing the rules on social etiquette.

I fed the group a meager meal and because our meal plans were dictated by what was defrosting that particular day, I withheld the steak dinner that we originally planned. I felt badly afterwards, especially when later in the week so many restaurants gave freely of their best meals and cuisines. I felt so ashamed of my selfishness that I could hardly enjoy my steak dinner when we finally ate it the next day. It was either that or the blister eruption discussion that ruined my appetite. When it was time to pass the bread, I declined my portion and passed it on.

It was from the teens' bike escapades that we learned the state of the city of Madison. We learned that tornado damage was just around the corner. The teenagers had also heard that WDRM was the only radio station on the air. This proved to be very helpful information as soon as we canvassed the neighborhood for eight-size D batteries to operate the only radio in the neighborhood. We were interested in hi-fi instead of Wi-fi. To watch neighbors hover over a small transistor radio reminded me of an old World War II movie, except the tornadoes replaced the bomb-toting war planes. We were going back to the basics.

Our social network of neighbors shared several generators. When it was our family's turn for generated power, I became excited about the possibility of a warm shower again. But it was not meant to be. Every other member of my household intercepted the power cords to charge their cell phones, on the off-chance that the cell towers had been restored. Phone coverage was sporadic, but every now and then, a lone text would come through and it would change the course of our day.

From the tidbits of texting information, we learned that friends' homes had been destroyed by the recent tornado invasion. Texting enabled us to assemble work groups to help the storm victims. Once we knew of a need, we were there. Counting on the teenage bikers to go from house-to-house gathering information was much like the gossip game we played in school. By the time the information got to the end of the line, the story was greatly exaggerated and sometimes didn't make sense. Instead, we counted on the teenagers to do what they did best: texting. Through their sharp texting abilities, we received the information in real-time and could act upon it more efficiently. The teens' social network was much faster than our word-of-mouth system and storm victims benefitted because of it.

Perhaps the largest impact of social media was seen in Tuscaloosa after the April 27th tornado disaster. Tuscaloosa was the bulls-eye of another deadly storm that same day. The debris was enough to fill the University of Alabama football stadium five times, according to Tuscaloosa's mayor, Walt Maddox. Funeral bells would toll 53 times for the citizens killed in Tuscaloosa after the six minute mammoth tornado ravaged the university town.

Tuscaloosa's emergency personnel told the students to stay away and the university faculty told the students to go home. Thankfully many innovative students decided to stay on the university's campus. Had it not been for their willingness to help, and their broad social connections, 10,500 meals would not have been distributed to storm victims and relief workers. Money, gift cards, diapers and other necessities would not have found their way into the hands of those that needed them if all the socially adept students had gone home. Finally, over 500 volunteers would not have been mobilized daily if the social network had not worked. Adults found themselves saying what they never thought they would say, "Thank goodness for cell phones and for kids who know how to use them."

In the *Find Your Passion* section of the University of Alabama's homepage, Chris Bryant tells of a student leader who used her sorority ties and Twitter account fans to launch an unprecedented effort called Greek Relief. Sororities teamed with fraternities to cook meals for victims and rescue workers in the fraternity's industrial-sized kitchen. The student originally had 150 Twitter followers. When she made a plea for help for Tuscaloosa, that number multiplied to 1000 and then exponentially to 4000 members within a few days. Local media re-tweeted her tweets and reached even more people willing to help the storm victims.

The students' relief effort went viral overnight. People around the nation could participate in Tuscaloosa's recovery and meet the city's deepest needs from afar. The Greek Relief motto became: "If you Tweet it, they will bring it." And indeed they did bring it. RVs full of food, supplies, and donations came from Nashville, and even Huntsville, which was among the storm-ridden cities. It was so typical of America that once Americans knew of a need, we would seek to meet it. People from Arizona followed Greek Relief on Twitter, and asked how they could help.

Young people from all over the tornado-harassed areas helped in the aftermath. Their willingness to show up, coupled with their social media skills and connections, transformed disaster relief into a well-oiled machine. Had I been the one in charge of organizing such an effort, I would still be unraveling a message, wondering if I was supposed to email it, text it, like it, tweet it or pin it. It was easier to holler up the stairs, "Can you hear me now?"

The social network is already making preparations for future disasters. Huntsville's own Bob Baron stepped up to the platform when the governor asked for measures that would save Alabama lives from another devastating weather catastrophe. In response, Baron Services introduced SAF-T-NET as a free service for Alabama residents. The service issues severe weather alerts up to fifteen minutes in advance of the approaching bad weather. Users receive either text messages or emails to alert them of pending storms so that they do not have to rely on weather radios or sirens that may not reflect storms in their immediate area. The weather alert service is manned 24/7 and can be programmed by the user to include up to four areas in Alabama for weather tracking.

My husband recently received a text message at 5:00 a.m. "Who in the world is texting you this early?" I asked. When he checked his message, it was a SAF-T-NET alert for one of the areas that he had programmed to receive notifications of threatening weather—our daughter's college location. We were able to warn her of the weather in case she didn't receive her own text notification. Since its inception, over 64,000 users have registered for the free SAF-T-NET weather notifications. That's potentially 64,000 lives that may be saved by early preparedness from future tornadoes. Mr. Baron was good on his word that no more tornadoes would slip by Huntsville, or any of his customers.

Not that any tornadoes would slip by us on April 27, 2011—the magnitude of tornado havoc was felt by most of Alabama. On April 26th, before the Day of Devastation, Baron's employee network could tell from the data that the parameters were coming together for another super outbreak. They fully anticipated this epic outbreak and Baron was very satisfied with his weather predicting radars and tools for public dissemination. He thought that every component worked as it was designed. The system worked. Alabama was prepared. This was a far cry from the limited storm data from 1989 that failed to produce a timely warning for those in the Huntsville storm's path years ago when Baron monitored the weather from a TV station.

Like most of North Alabama on April 27th, Baron Services lost power during the storm's fury. One generator kept the weather operations going for seven days before power finally returned. It was one of the few ways that people could stay connected with the weather. When his staff reviewed the storm data from April 27th, Mr. Baron told me how pleased he was with the algorithms and began to go into detail about the figures and statistics before he noticed the blank look on my face. Then he succinctly summed it up and said, "I was very impressed with the coordination and organization."

Baron also stated that the first responders and the Emergency Management Agency were top-notch. Speaking of the coordination effort in Madison County, he said, "Things were done properly here.

We did it right." Information was disseminated to the public in the timeliest manner possible and all branches of public service coordinated with one another very well. When I asked Mr. Baron what was next for Baron Services regarding technology, he said, "We'll continue to keep up with the new technology and ever-changing ways that people get information."

Being engrossed in social media was worth it during Alabama's tornado aftermath. The social network protected us, informed us, brought people together, aided the relief effort, and resulted in changed lives. I finally saw the power of social media and connection, although I did not understand how to use all of the information at my fingertips. However, mastering social media skills was probably an easier feat than getting my children to accept their own mother as a friend on Facebook.

Shelly Van Meter Miller

20
UNDER SIEGE

A crisis brought out the extremes, the best and the worst in people; hence givers and takers. Perfect strangers lent a hand, performing chores that were left undone around their own homes. I scrubbed a stranger's refrigerator after the storm although my own was in different stages of growing penicillin. People came out of the woodwork with chainsaws, sweet tea, and even special tornado cupcakes--anything to help in the relief effort of the tornado aftermath. Stopping only to mop the Alabama humidity off of their brow, the givers went beyond the call of duty to help their next door neighbors or the unfortunate storm victims who lived just down the street.

While extraordinary good will was exchanged, perfect strangers and nearby neighbors also robbed each other blind. During a catastrophe, the term was "looting," but any other day, it was called stealing. Thieves sought the tornado devastated areas as a playground to wreak more havoc than the storm. They could get away with the perfect crime and the tornado would take the brunt of the blame. A White House Chief of Staff once said, "You should never waste a good crisis." Such was the criminal mentality after April's deadly tornadoes. These were the takers who showed up in full force for their "gimmees."

Mother Nature was blamed for crimes she didn't commit. A twister could have easily taken the computer and the flat screen TV when it took the roof and the front yard trees. The storm victims were already devastated. Home owners were distracted, shedding their guard against these thieves that called in the night. No alarm systems, no phone service, 911 disabled, law enforcement preoccupied—it was a hell raiser's heyday!

In an effort to protect their citizens, the city officials acted swiftly. A curfew of 7:00 p.m. was enacted immediately. Those caught after hours were arrested on the spot. In Alabama, we clung to our guns and our religion. You either owned a shotgun, or you owned multiple shotguns, in addition to wasp spray. If criminals didn't learn their lessons through vigilante means, we could still hunt them down after they were in prison. Many churches supported a prison ministry and sought converts from a "captive" audience. Both guns and religion could be used as weapons. We called it spiritual warfare. I didn't know why anyone would choose to be a criminal in Alabama, especially on the stark, dark night of April 27th, because both guns and wasp canisters were fully loaded.

Our friends from church lost their home at 4:47 p.m. that fateful April day, and by 9:00 p.m. they slept under a canopy of stars while inside their home. Only one room withstood the storm while their roof was on someone else's house. A constellation became their view overhead. Along with the stars, they slept with their loaded gun, prepared to protect their fragmented property. Neighbors took turns keeping watch in the night. Generators powered the previously stored Christmas tree lights that the tornado dropped from various attics. Not much was left on Yarbrough Road, so the twinkling lights merely decorated the debris while attempting to ward off looters.

Providing assistance to the worst-hit areas required arm bands to enter the neighborhoods, ensuring that helpers had a purpose instead of canvassing for looting opportunities. Law enforcement officials blocked intersections for arm band checks. The banding sometimes stood in the way of progress because the limited drop points were overly crowded. All good works would come to an end by the 7:00 p.m. curfew hour.

Alabama's governor sent 1400 National Guard troops to stand sentry over the roads that led to the most heavily damaged neighborhoods. When a friend's home was trampled by one of the tornadoes, we decided to drive our truck since the truck could handle the impassable roads and storm debris better than our family car, which had another flat tire. Flying tornado debris had hit my car tire, instead of vice versa. I was famous for my flat tires.

It was a good thing the ole truck had enough gas to get us to the country, for every gas station in the county was closed for lack of electricity. In nearby Athens where the gas was still pumping, the lines were longer than they were during the Jimmy Carter days. My neighbors tried to siphon gas from their John Deere lawnmower, but it didn't go well.

We inched forward as the traffic snaked along the highway. Sitting up higher in the truck, I saw one long conga line of vehicles ahead. The sun beamed through the windshield showing a fine stream of dust particles floating above the dashboard. There was nothing else to do but sit and wait, and hope that we didn't run out of gas before we could help our friend. I didn't realize it at the time, but the traffic wait would be our only opportunity to rest that day.

We continued to drive our Chevy truck down Highway 72 past other truck drivers. The truckers mimicked one another's driving styles with one hand on top of the steering wheel. Holding onto their steering wheels, they flicked their hand in a subtle way, meant as a wave, when another truck passed. "Who was that?" I asked. It was just another truck. Truck drivers flicked their wrists casually to illustrate the truck bond. No one else did this while driving. I never waved to other Volvos, so it was definitely a truck thing.

Near the turn-off to our friend's home, the road was blocked by an armored truck and two National Guardsmen with rifles strapped across their chests. Cars made U-turns in the middle of the highway, turned away by the guards. We inched forward, dreading the desolation that awaited us and the red tape of getting through the roadblock. When we closed in on the guards, my husband rolled down his truck window. I slid across the seat, ready to plead our case of why they should let us pass. In my peripheral vision, I saw my husband's hand on the steering wheel lift for the hand flick maneuver. The guardsman flick waved at the same time and waved us through toward our destination. Because of the truck bond, we kept right on truckin'.

Our laughter subsided after two blocks as we inhaled a deep breath when we saw the shocking display on both sides of the road. It took all of our attention to drive the narrow path that was supposed to be the road. I tried not to stare as despair and misery stared back. Immediately I knew which people were homeowners, or rather, former homeowners. They were the ones with zombie-like stares, too numb to realize that they were the center of attention.

In the backseat, my daughter held her cell phone at eye level, prepared to snap a picture of the desert of desolation. "Put that away," I interjected. My memory took me back years to when my Uncle Peter's crushed vehicle was displayed on the busiest street of my hometown. Rubberneckers passed the metal heap and exclaimed, "There's no way anyone could have lived through that!" They were right. My uncle didn't make it. When our funeral procession passed on the way to the cemetery, carrying Uncle Peter in a different car, we were forced to view his demolished car. When Uncle Peter's brothers confronted the mechanic at the car shop, he tossed them a remnant from the crashed vehicle. It was a tennis shoe--only one. What a painful leftover. I found myself repeating the same thing forty years later upon staring at the heaps left by the EF4 tornado: "There's no way anyone could have lived through that." Those people must not have been home when the tornado uncoiled on top of their house.

Blank foundations were surrounded by shards of mismatched bricks that didn't belong to the same home. The bricks may have been dumped by the tornado from a different town, possibly as far away as Hackleburg, AL. People carted things to and fro, bumping into one another like busy ants. Some people just stood still, confused by the chaos.

I found myself staring and couldn't pull away from the rolled down window. I did not want to accidentally make eye contact with a homeowner. Tears welled up and there was no mistaking the pity on my face, or the way I winced when I saw something bizarre in the rubble. A solitary shoe could evoke a myriad of emotions from someone hurting. I did not want to add more pain to the victims' lives. As much as they deserved pity, storm victims weren't interested in it. They were interested in our help for their community that was currently under siege.

It was difficult to know where to begin, but our friends definitely needed us and there was no turning back. With the guardsmen's guns mounted behind us and the land stripped as if a bomb detonated, the region resembled scenes from the movie, The Apocalypse. It was the same across most of Alabama. Entire neighborhoods lay in ruins from the tornado aftermath. I shut my eyes to the mismatched shoes and put on heavy-duty gloves. It was time to go to work.

21
BAD GRADES

Even a kindergartner knew that numbers and letters didn't mix. My five-year-old brother came home from school to inform our mother that his buddy, Brad misspelled his own name. My brother couldn't spell either, so my mother wondered how he knew whether Brad's name was incorrectly spelled. "Because it had the number 4 in it," my brother answered. Just when you thought you were smarter than a five year old! Names weren't supposed to have numbers in them.

I thought about telling that to my eighth grade algebra teacher. After staring at a problem and hoping that it would grow wings and fly off the page, I waited for a lull in the line to speak with the math teacher. Back then, we received teacher assistance but only if the teacher didn't have to move. We really stood in line to steal a glimpse at the teacher's manual. Some only wanted to double-check their correct answers and receive a pat on the back. I was not one of them. When the teacher looked at my eraser marks that literally dug a hole in the problem, he mumbled, "You can't mix apples and oranges." Apples and oranges referred to x's and exponents. From then on, I kept my eye out for things that didn't mix and match.

I knew when I saw a large X spray painted on the muddied siding of a wrecked home with numbers intersecting the letter that something was wrong. The bright orange X was FEMA's international symbol of a search-and-rescue mission. FEMA's website explains the initials, numbers, and date that were chalked on the X angles. It reminded me of bad grades. Worse than that, the numbers mixed with letters weren't imaginary apples and oranges, but rather an indication of life or death.

Zero was ideal. I was relieved to see the bright orange X with a zero (0) beside it, meaning no victims were found during the search. If fatalities were found, that number increased and was written as such: 2-live, 3-dead. For a home which was flattened by a tornado, no structure was left on which to draw the X. Many fatalities occurred when houses collapsed, so there would be no X's although there would be deaths. Only the semi-intact houses had a 2" X 2" letter X displayed near their entrances.

A single slash / meant that a search was in progress. The completed X meant the home was already searched. Trained rescuers marked all entry points. A square indicated that an entry was safe. But a square with an X in the box meant that it was not safe to enter. Sometimes the initials, HM, stood for 'hazardous material.' I never saw such initials, but did notice, "Gas Leak" spray painted next to an X. The date and military time was listed in chalk as well as the specialist's ID who performed the search.

More bad grades were embedded in tornado jargon, forming combinations like EF4 or EF5. Those groupings were lethal. They stood for the Enhanced Fujita scale, named after the doctor who invented it. A version of Dr. Ted Fujita's scale was first used after the 1974 tornado outbreak. The scale was enhanced in 2007, making it less subjective to grade tornadoes. A tornado received a grade based on wind speed and damage. NOAA's Storm Prediction Center produced a scale from 0-5 with the higher the number, the worse the grade. An EF4 meant wind speed was between 166-200 mph. An EF5 rating was reserved for the more violent tornadoes with winds over 200 mph. Both EF4 and EF5 tornadoes were considered, "violent, significant, and intense." In other words, they were deadly.

The *Weather Channel's* exclusive TOR:CON rating was the newest combination of letters and numbers. On April 27, 2011, the entire state of Alabama was given a rating of TOR:CON 10, the worst level. It meant that Alabama had a 100% chance of a tornado striking within a fifty mile radius on that day. The Tornado Condition scale was designed by Dr. Greg Forbes of *The Weather Channel* who studied under Dr. Fujita. Dr. Forbes discovered that a hook echo displayed on a radar screen indicated the strongest tornado. He was correct when posting the tornado bulls-eye on Alabama. Twisters were poised as darts with our state as the dartboard. Even with a TOR:CON 10, no one could imagine that over sixty tornadoes would come at us like a bat pounding a piñata until our possessions burst and spilled over the state. The FEMA X, the Enhanced Fujita scale, the Tornado Condition Index—all were tornado symbols for bad grades. Alabama received failing grades in all three categories on April 27, 2011. Extreme grades meant tornado raids.

Shelly Van Meter Miller

22
THE LAND DOWN UNDER

I thought once inside the church, the chaos would simmer down. After all, it was two days after the April 27th tornadoes had unleashed their terror. Even more powerful than the violent winds, good will and neighborly love unleashed with people falling over one another to assist the victims. I stood in line at the Good Shepherd Church basement, waiting to sign up to work the shelter. I waved to my friend working the desk. "I didn't know you went to church here," I stated while searching for an open slot to register.

"I'm just helping out," she answered. And so was I. All slots were taken, so I shuffled from room to room to see which one needed help. A line wrapped around the corner and funneled into one open door, obviously the food line. My mouth watered when I saw happy people exiting with their folded Chick-fil-A bags out the same door where others entered. A white sack with red letters whisked past me and I caught the aroma of the chicken nuggets and the tangy Polynesian sauce. Then it hit me: I had withdrawals from fast food, which meant that I couldn't even go two days without something fried. Because of the power outage, we either grilled or cooked on the fire pit whatever happened to be in the freezer, nothing fast or fried. I was thankful for our provisions but would've been more thankful had I had my own white sack of nuggets. I turned a deaf ear to my stomach groans and chose self-control over gluttony. It was all I could do not to join the food line. Besides, my friend already recognized me.

Every room was a flurry of activity. The bathrooms and showers were all in use, along with a kitchen and cots too. I never knew all this existed in the church basement. It was an underground village, its own community after the tornado devastation. I waded into the gym which was a makeshift warehouse. Hordes of clothes were heaped almost to the rims of the basketball goals. Good Shepherd hosted Upwards basketball for elementary children and that was how the church came to be the safe haven after the tornadoes. All games were cancelled, but the concession stand was open for business. Volunteers figured that if they could run a concession stand for the ballgames, they could cater to the community and feed the hungry. The church started with a few boxes of Skittles, Ring pops and Three Musketeers—the equivalent to two fish and five loaves of bread. They may not have fed five thousand, but they could have. The first night, sixty stranded victims were housed and fed at the church. The second night they sheltered and fed twenty-eight, and for the next eleven days, eleven storm victims called the church their home. This gave new meaning to 'finding a church home.' For the time being, it was their only home.

Even those who weren't official 'storm victims' were cared for at the church. Some came from South Huntsville just for the food. Although no tornadoes touched the southern part of town, the power outage still left residents without food and nowhere to buy it. The church welcomed all who were hungry or homeless, including FEMA workers. The government agency came to assist storm victims, but had to stay two hours away in Birmingham because no hotel rooms were available in the storm-damaged areas. The church basement had additional cots and invited FEMA workers to sleep in the same shelter as the tornado victims.

Other churches joined the concession stand effort and the casserole brigade brought in more troops—church ladies from all over the tornado-plagued area. Dominoes, Publix, Atlanta Bread and Newks restaurant also fed the hungry from Good Shepherd Church's concession stand. The church shelter was one of the few places where you could get a hot meal. One generator kept the refrigerator running while four other generators controlled the lights and the water heater. The generators were gifts, the courtesy of another Methodist church in Leper's Fork, TN. Upon hearing that a fellow Methodist church was in need, the Tennessee church arrived in

Alabama at 6:30 a.m. the morning following the epic tornadoes. Church volunteers from the Volunteer State promptly delivered generators, gas, coolers and chainsaws.

One of the church basement rooms that I ventured into during my work shift was the "chainsaw room." It was the smallest room with two men, chainsaws, and a table inside. One of the men eagerly greeted me at the door and asked if I came to saw or to be sawed. I had heard of "see or be seen," but he was referring to whether I wanted to help chainsaw or if I needed someone to do it for me. It was not unusual in Alabama for a female to operate a chainsaw. While a Northern lady might ask for a North Face jacket or Isotoner slippers for gifts, a Southern woman would ask for a new gun or a chainsaw. One of my best friends received a chainsaw for Christmas and couldn't wait to use it, so I let her cut down an old pine tree in my backyard that had been struck by lightning. She did an exceptional cutting job, but we both forgot the effort it took to haul away the dead tree. The chainsaw worked great. I asked for a new wheelbarrow for Mother's Day to finish the job.

Back in the basement's chainsaw room, I mumbled that I stumbled into the wrong room. I realized after walking away that I had met members of the chain gang. Their work would not end when the concessions ran out and the shelter shut down. Their chainsaw ministry would continue into summer's sweltering months, changing lives with each fallen tree—like on the day they encountered Sonny and his mess.

Shelly Van Meter Miller

23
SONNY AND THE GENERAL

The members of the chainsaw gang were exhausted, drenched in sweat, and craving Chick-fil-A after their confrontation with several misplaced trees on Clutts Road. The men packed their chainsaws in the back of the pick-up before heading to their next chainsaw assignment. A stop at the church shelter for a hot meal was in order first. The men could see the church gleaming in the distance like an oasis in the tornado-ravaged grassland. It was easier to see now because there were fewer trees in the way. The town of Harvest was missing one of its finest features: shade.

The chain gang volunteers passed a single home along the way, and saw a man swinging a miniature chainsaw against a massive tree trunk that stretched across the driveway. The men knew what they had to do. I wonder if they realized that some of life's most important events happen while on the way to somewhere else. That had to be it because the timing was really bad.

Sonny stood in his blocked driveway watching as three men stepped from the vehicle and reached into the truck, brandishing three powerful chainsaws. Sonny did not mean to be standoffish as they approached him, "I'm good!" he hollered. The work that lay before Sonny was overwhelming, but it was his house and he was a proud man. He had lived alone since he could remember and doubted whether his own family knew of his recent tornado encounter. He barely remembered the details himself. First he was thrown against the kitchen wall, suspended as if a giant magnet pulled him into the drywall. After it dropped him in a heap, he wasn't sure how long he lay curled on the kitchen floor linoleum.

He reminded himself that he was a Purple Heart recipient and that he didn't need the do-gooders strolling up his driveway with their fancy tools. They were probably from the church up the road. But the chainsaw gang fired up their saws and drowned out his protests. They meant to clear his driveway before they earned their soul food at the church headquarters.

Sonny was too tired to battle and possibly still shell-shocked, so he let them do it. When the Good Samaritans sawed their way up the drive, all engines sputtered to a stop when Sonny's house came into view. An even larger tree went through Sonny's roof and came out the other side like Cupid's arrow. It was time to call in the big guns.

Additional crews volunteered to roof Sonny's house. But like so many things, one thing led to another, and before the house could support a new roof, the structure needed extensive work. Miraculously, a company out of Florence, AL donated a travel trailer to the church up the road, which then donated it to Sonny as a temporary home. The volunteer work crew was making great progress on Sonny's house when the pastor of the church 'up the road' received a phone call from Redstone Arsenal.

A three-star general was visiting Huntsville for a retirement party and wished to tour the tornado-damaged region. Would the church be so kind as to host the general and his entourage for a day while he visited with the needy? The work crews groaned. They had serious work to do and no one wanted to worry about a tag-along VIP interested in a photo-op. Visions of a soldier in a decorated uniform, posing with a soup ladle half-raised while serving the food line flashed through the volunteer's heads, or the general cranking up their good chainsaws while cameras flashed. Patting their pastor on the back, the chainsaw gang concurred, "Pastor David, babysitting the general is a pastoral duty."

The pastor was stuck with 'General duty,' but felt that the photo shoots wouldn't last long. He was wrong. The general allotted over four hours from his busy schedule, skipping the watered down version of the grand tornado tour and proceeded to get his hands dirty. The general sat down to breakfast with storm victims and listened to their stories. And then he got to work. The volunteers were dumfounded and for once, their pastor was speechless when the three-star general ended his phone call with Korea and asked how he could best serve Alabama.

"I guess we could take him to Sonny's house," one volunteer offered, "but I'm not going to be the one to tell Sonny." That was another one of those pastoral duties. Pastor David was chosen to approach Sonny regarding the General's wishes.

"Ain't no way a three-star general gonna work on my home," cried Sonny unworthily.

No one wanted the general. The volunteers assumed that the visit was an ego-boosting, political baby-kissing, and photo-op outing for the general. Sonny didn't feel deserving that a person in the general's position would stoop to work on his modest house. But the general was intent on what the general wanted to do, and worked side-by-side with Sonny in the dusty worksite, talking of old times like they were good buddies. Coincidentally, they had served together at the same fort in Kansas.

During a work break, Sonny sheepishly asked the camera crew for a picture with the general. He thought some more and boldly asked for another picture, this time with the general and the house in the background, maybe to prove the general really came to his house, and it wasn't a dream. By the end of the stay, Sonny shamelessly chased after the general's auto fleet for just one more picture of him and the general hugging. Sonny felt his life was complete although his house wasn't.

He continued to reside in the travel trailer as his house progressed. Sonny grew used to the do-gooders and appreciated their assistance, so much that when FEMA came through with $10K in aid for him, Sonny donated the money to those whose needs were greater. He regularly stopped by the church just to chat and grew closer to his family. Two weeks before Sonny's move-in date, Pastor David received another phone call.

It was Sonny's mother. Sonny had passed away in his trailer. His mother asked for the pastor to come to the trailer. As Pastor David stepped inside, Sonny appeared to be sleeping in his usual chair. "I just wanted you to see how peaceful Sonny went to his eternal rest," Sonny's mother broke the silence. As he looked at Sonny's serene face, the pastor noticed a picture of Sonny and the general just above the chair. The end table next to the chair displayed another picture of Sonny and the general, taken just days after the tornado. Finally, the last picture of Sonny hugging the general was directly where Sonny could best see it, along with the newly framed copy of a Purple Heart certificate that the general sent to Sonny after his visit. Now Sonny's life was complete.

24
LIKE A GOOD NEIGHBOR

"Our cul-de-sac is so boring," my children moaned. Good, because I liked boring. Boring was one of my top three requirements when choosing a neighborhood. Boring meant sipping lemonade while relaxing with my cat on the screened porch, or floating around the pool on an inner tube while reading a racy book. Boring meant lounging on the hammock in the shade, or sitting on the dock and dipping my feet into the lake. I chose boring on purpose and pretended our backyard lake was actually Walden Pond. If only it had been a toy gun that my neighbors shot at me from across the lake.

There was no mistaking the gun shot ricocheting off of the rocked embankment and zipping into the lake, past my dangling feet. "Hey!" I shouted. "Who shot at me?" The bushes shook as the shooter hid from sight. A father figure emerged and retorted, "You talkin' to me?" but his Southern drawl didn't have the same tone as the famous movie line.

"You bet I was! Don't do it again!" I retorted. Ph-ew-ew! And there it went again. This time I was calling the police. By the time the police rounded the lake, the 'McCoys' vacated the premises. The officers asked what type of gun the shooters used and expected me to know. Did anyone really ask what kind of gun someone was using to shoot at them? I later found the remains from an airsoft rifle but it was too late because the famous battle of the Hatfields and the McCoys was already being reenacted in our small, suburban neighborhood. I was a 'Hatfield,' just minding my own business, while a 'McCoy' missed the ducks and instead took a shot at me from across the lake. My plans for a boring neighborhood were then "shot out of the water," so to speak.

Not everyone in our neighborhood shot at their neighbors. Usually our cul-de-sac banded together against bandits. On one quiet day, a window salesman, late for his sales call, left a message on my answering machine, "Seven police cars barred the entrance to your street because of the bank robber on the loose..." I replayed the message when suddenly the doorbell rang. I fumbled for the wasp spray and placed my finger on the trigger. But it was my neighbor, bringing a new cat toy for Kitty. I cracked the door with my lips protruding through the tiny opening, "Go Home! There's a robber in the neighborhood!" With that, I slammed the door in her face and turned the dead bolt. She made it home before the high speed chase ended when the robber drove his stolen car into a fence. If not for the fence, the stolen car would have been gurgling in the neighbor's swimming pool. The robber then fled on foot with hundred dollar bills in his wake. His apprehension made the top story on the local news and reporters noted that most of the money was recovered. Fellow neighbors had the same idea and searched around the fence, even digging into the neighbor's mulch pile just in case some bills strayed to the heap. No such luck.

Neighbors mostly kept to themselves except during robberies and target practice. We apologized for locking one another out and pulled together when it counted. At those rare times, we morphed into a little village and depended on our neighbors to get us through the current crisis, the epic blackout after the tornadoes of April 2011.

Helen Keller said this now famous quote: "I would rather walk with a friend in the dark, than alone in the light." Ms. Keller hit the nail on the head and didn't dream that she would be describing the scene of fellow Alabama residents a half-century after her famous quote. Never did a truer sentiment describe the power outage caused by the killer tornadoes. Neighbors came together and pooled their possessions for the common good so that no one would walk through the dark alone. Seven generators kept our freezer contents frozen and our cell phones charged. The number of generators on our cul-de-sac was the same number used by the Browns Ferry Nuclear Power Plant.

We shared food, batteries, ice and gas. We also shared good ideas like using outdoor solar lights as torches in the middle of the night, and helpful hygienic secrets as well. Although our sense of sight was dulled, our sense of smell was not. The idea was to wash laundry in the bathtub. After dumping detergent in the bath water, my daughter and I sloshed the clothes around with our feet, simulating the wash cycle. Visions of Lucy and Ethel squashing grapes came to mind. Washing clothes was never so much fun. However, we were a sorry excuse for a rinse cycle, for when our newly laundered garments were worn and happened to get wet, the clothes frequently foamed at the knees.

During the power outage, every evening was spent with neighbors around the fire pit. We fanned the flames well into the night, and lingered until the last embers died. It was then that we stared to the heavens and saw constellations that were never before seen from our neighborhood. Thousands of tiny sequins pricked the sky and reminded me of reading about the time when the stars fell on Alabama. When the fire was finally snuffed out, we carried our solar torches upstairs to bed like Wee Willy Winkies in our nightgowns. When my head hit the pillow, I smelled the fire pit smoke in my hair. How long could I pretend to camp out in my own house?

One of the powerless days, the McCoys pulled their boat ashore. I instinctively held my hands up and longed for my wasp spray, wondering if it really could spray twenty feet. The shooters said, "If the city shuts off our water, we have kegs full of fresh water if you need some." With that, they rowed back to their side of the lake. I lowered my hands slightly to wave goodbye. Was it possible that the power outage was powerful enough to call a truce between the Hatfields and McCoys? And could the tornado enforce a cease-fire? It would take more than 62 tornado tracks to end the Alabama rivalry. As soon as the power came on, it was game on! That was how I knew that life would return to normal. So much for boring.

When I thought of neighbors, I didn't just think of the shooters. I thought of those on either side of my house, neighbors that I could borrow a cup of sugar from, or buy a crate of oranges from their son in the band if they bought a cheesecake from my daughter's soccer team. We exchanged so many high-priced favors from countless fundraisers that I felt like posting a sign in our yard stating: No soliciting unless you have Thin Mints. But that wouldn't be very neighborly.

During April's tornadoes, we found who our true neighbors were. One man in Madison County was hit during the early morning round of twisters and found over thirty fallen trees in his yard. None of them were his. For days, the same tree removal crew labored to restore his property. The owner was surprised to learn that the volunteer crew was from Nashville, TN, over two hours away. The Tennessee volunteers explained, "When Nashville flooded the year before, the government was a no-show, but Alabama showed up to help. That's why we're here—to repay a favor." The week of the storms, the border state of Tennessee was like a next door neighbor.

That week was one of the few times that the South was relieved to hear that the Yankees were coming. Thank goodness for the Yankees and their power crews, generators, ice bags, bottled water, batteries, and storage pods. They thought of everything we needed and everything we didn't know we needed. Even Yankees from as far north as Wisconsin drove to a state they'd never stepped foot in before. Trucks from Illinois delivered supplies and then turned around for the long drive back home. We later found that the driver of one of those semi-trucks was a high school classmate of my husband's from Marion, IL. She did not know we lived in Alabama at the time of the tornadoes, but remembered what it was like to lose one of their mutual classmates in the Marion tornado thirty years ago. Tornado victims would always share a common bond and many times that link would prompt them to reach out to complete strangers, even decades later.

Northerners assisted us in every aspect and in ways that we could never repay. They stayed to do the dirty work and saw Alabama at its worst, but its citizens at their best. Even so, we could not have recovered on our own. We found that strangers hundreds of miles away were our neighbors. As a certain commercial goes, like a good neighbor, they were there.

RECOVERY

25
THE TOWN CRIER

"Hear ye, Hear ye," the town crier rang his bell. "It's six o' clock and all is well." Six months had passed since a colossal tornado outbreak flattened parts of Alabama and all was not well, the people cried. Lives still smoldered as did the burn piles. Lost loved ones were sorely missed and both family and neighbors were split apart. Many neighbors chose not to rebuild or could not afford to, others battled with insurance settlements. One man died before resolving insurance woes. Vacant lots broke up the landscape and "For Sale" signs sprung up on top of the debris piles. The Ground Zero appearance had zero curb appeal. Vultures circled above the forsaken land, spinning an aerial bulls-eye over the forlorn countryside where the eye of the storm circled six months earlier.

I drove up and down the street three times but didn't recognize the area where I had once sifted through my friend's belongings, trying to salvage the remnants of her life. She survived the tornado by fleeing her home when the tornado approached. Her home did not survive, nor did much of her stuff. I felt foolish on my third round of cruising, searching for a house that didn't exist. I was sure the folks at the end of the lane were amused by my third U-turn. By now, they were accustomed to gawkers and probably regretted not charging admission. A hand-painted sign in their front yard stated, "Thanks to all who helped." An American flag waved proudly on a pole beside the sign. The folks on the front porch waved as well. Although it looked like a bomb went off, I felt at home where both the flags and the people still waved.

At the same time, I prayed that I didn't acquire my fifth flat tire for 2011. My ongoing record was six flats in a year, and I didn't want to break any records while in tornado territory. I counted the concrete slabs that blended in with the sky. There was so much sky. Out of some foundations grew thriving pokeberry bushes taller than any of the limbless trees that barely hung onto life. Just when I was about to give up, I saw it protruding from the heap. I hoisted myself in the driver's seat to peer over the debris pile to see a lone fireplace and chimney that shielded the glare of the sun.

The living room fireplace was only useful for roasting marshmallows now. My friends knew how to take the lemons that the tornado tossed them and make lemonade. The chimney was all that was left of the home that they built themselves. They still visited the property, hoping that each time would be a little less painful. Nothing was as difficult and emotional for them as when the bulldozer shoved their home into a large mound for the next day's trash pick-up. They had watched the walls tumble down. Their cat of seventeen years repeatedly ran back into the house as it was being demolished and work crews had waited while my friends retrieved their cat. The cat survived the tornado and the house demolition, and always looked both ways before crossing the street, but he was no match for the constant traffic that beat down the road to view the tornado aftermath, gawkers like me.

When my brother was young, he loved everything that had to do with construction and didn't miss an episode of *Bob the Builder*. He would have been in his element on Yarbrough Road! I saw a bunch of builders, some possibly named Bob. Construction crews were plentiful and the tornado shelter business was booming. Home sales were stagnant, but once a sign advertised the free tornado shelter that came with the house, the home sold by the end of the week. In certain areas, like the one I was currently lost in, progress was slow and the neighbors still reeled from the scars that were inflicted for six minutes one Wednesday afternoon. Thieves regularly visited the reconstructed houses to steal the copper wiring. One thief was caught red-handed when his get-away car caught fire. Firefighters opened his trunk to put out the blaze and were amazed to find a whole neighborhood's worth of copper wiring. One house alone had $5000 worth of installed copper wiring stolen from it. The story reminded me of "Liar, Liar, pants on fire."

Even while playing soccer nearby, players found it difficult to see the goal through the haze of smoke that billowed from the field across the way. The never-ending burn piles were still the norm. Paul Gattis from *The Huntsville Times* reported on October 25, 2011, that 337 sites already had storm debris removed which added up to 246 tons. That didn't count the tons that had gone up in smoke. Owners were tired of staring at the remains which were constant reminders of the ruin. One homeowner finally posted a sign on a massive tree stump which had an army of roots: Please take me. The debris trucks drove past the stump for months and must have thought it was yard art.

Back on the road, I turned the corner to the Harvest House restaurant and recalled the hot, juicy, hamburger patty that was handed to me after I shucked my work gloves. Both victims and volunteers were blessed during the tornado recovery by the generosity of local businesses which fired up the grills and fed us. Driving one block further, everything was picture-perfect. Only steps away from dead trees and empty foundations, the homes that were unaffected by the storms remained intact and were decorated with fall wreaths, pumpkins and pansies.

The sound of rustling leaves was now absent as were the trees, but the October skies and crisp breezes announced a new season with fall and the coming of Halloween. This time of year, our cul-de-sac crew once again gathered like the homeless around fire pits set in the middle of the street. We surrounded the pits with our lawn chairs, tailgating for trick-or-treaters. Most likely the tradition began because we were too lazy to answer our doors to Halloween callers. Instead we stationed buckets of candy around our chairs while children circled us like frenzied sharks, some circling more than once.

As part of our Halloween tradition, we exchanged good gossip which inevitably led to politics. We decided that one of our neighbors needed to run for mayor and spent the evening persuading him or her to run for office. The 'candidate' was assured that he would be a shoo-in within our neighborhood. We threatened to write his name on the ballot anyway and addressed him as, "Mr. Mayor" for the rest of the night. Our nighttime chatter reminded the fire pit crew of the last time the neighbors gathered around a fire.

It was the day after the tornadoes fell on Alabama. The memory brought mixed emotions, some strangely peaceful and some intensely jarring. In April our fire pit was both stove and heater when we lost power. We cooked on the carport instead of cooking in the middle of the street. We gathered together and pooled resources so that each meal was a Mulligan Stew concoction with each neighbor tossing something in the pot. While reminiscing, someone in our circle mentioned that it had been a fun week after the tornadoes. There was an awkward silence as soon as the words were spoken. I sensed that same awkward moment many times since April 27th. It was guilt—guilt because we dined on steaks and pork tenderloin and other contents of our deep freezers, while neighbors lost their deep freezer, along with the rest of their belongings. It was guilt because our fire pits were mobile while friends were left with only a chimney, now their pit. It was guilt for napping on a hammock, relaxing even with the buzz of chain saws and ambulance sirens. It was guilt because we had been in the right place at the right time. We were guilty of being lucky. Finally we felt guilty for spending a satisfying week with loved ones while members of our community lost loved ones and spent their week searching for a place with electricity to hold a funeral.

I hid my guilt for six months. Finally on Halloween night, someone expressed the unmentionable, that "it" had been a good week. My feelings were normal, it turned out. We said goodbye to "Mr. Mayor" and promised to return next year to the same spot unless another tornado drew us together first.

I made my final round of tornado territory and drove past several trunk-or-treat advertisements which attempted to lure children to church with candy. Trick-or-treaters could hop from church to church and then from trunk to trunk, reaping rewards of ghoulish goodies. One church sign read: "Today is a gift. That's why it's called the present." We could all say, "Amen!" to that.

26
I NEVER PROMISED YOU A ROSE GARDEN

I wasn't expecting a rose garden, but this? Ten months ago, 62 syncopated tornadoes wreaked havoc on our state and reduced regions to ruins. I smelled the tornado ruins before I encountered them. The fumes from countless burn piles lingered in the air. I wondered what could possibly be left to burn from almost a year ago.

The woodless woods looked like an Alabama chainsaw massacre. Naturalists made up a new word and tried to recover a remnant of beauty among the carcasses of downed trees. Those beheaded trees had an actual name called "snags." A snag was another word for a dead tree. Limbless trees or totem poles were more descriptive names that provided a good habitat for birds and other wildlife. The snags were stopping places for creatures on their way to somewhere more beautiful, but certainly not this place.

A tree expert saw the snags in an interesting light. When asked if the trees should be eliminated, the tree expert replied, "You could leave them, but they (the trees) might be embarrassed." He was right. They were naked without their leaves and branches. The splintered trees stood as grave markers for homes that once graced the property. The homeowners weren't coming back and neither were the ancient hardwood trees. The snags and the empty foundations were all that remained.

Even while driving through the area at night, I could see the eerie silhouettes of the trees and knew immediately that I had entered "The Tornado Zone." The trees stood like useless sentinels in the empty fields. Their barren branches hung with drooping kudzu which was the only thing that kept the partially uprooted trees standing. The former forest may as well have been a swamp in a bayou instead of a woodland.

In April 2011, thousands of hardwood trees died in a matter of minutes. The trees were 'older than the hills.' Most were snapped in the storm's frenzy or uprooted and yanked out of the ground, roots and all. Other trees weren't given any mercy. They remained in the ground, but the tornadoes had left them so misshapen, while others had their bark blown apart by the intense pressure of the storm, exposing the trees' natural feeding tubes. Those trees would die a slow death by starvation. Eventually, a dull thud vibrated the ground and signaled that another one had bitten the dust as a tree gave up its fight and collapsed on top of the others.

My husband and I searched the desolate property where a spacious ranch home once stood. We counted gravel paths to make sure we were on the correct piece of land first. Then we took the long driveway up the embankment to an empty foundation, expecting to find old cinderblocks for a project. There were none in sight. Some daffodils tried to poke through the briars, but they only decorated the dullness. Monkey grass lined the sidewalk to the porch where one had existed. Now the grass weaved a path to nowhere. It wasn't until we reached the top of the drive and looked down towards the ravine that we saw a concrete jungle swallowed by thorny briars, with chunks of cinderblocks poking up through the red mud, much like a rural Stonehenge.

I saw what they meant by snags. Trees had snagged pieces of metal that now decorated what was left of their limbs. The branches clawed out to seize anything that blew past them during last April's storms. Edgar Allen Poe could have found his muse here for another dismal novel setting. There was even a raven among the snags, guarding a plunder of debris. I tried to picture how the ravine looked before, at the bottom of a tree-filled hill, with flowing water babbling over mossy rocks, the banks surrounded with wildflowers. Now it was a burial ground for concrete. The scene was now colorless except for the black Raven whose cry was almost human, threatening to accost us if we drew closer. We were in the dead of winter and didn't expect a lush, green valley. However, now it seemed the land would not "go green" again. All hope was buried when the bulldozer hurled the condemned home and its contents over the cliff.

Not all hope was gone for the owner of the adjacent property. After the storms damaged a fellow gardener's property, a group of Master Gardeners donated heirloom plants from their own gardens and sowed a rich vegetable and herb garden for the property owner. There was nothing that anyone could do for the house or the dead trees, but gardeners could do what gardeners do: they could plant a garden. Although the tornado-damaged home was unlivable for six months after the storm, and its trees were twisted into various pretzel shapes, one potted tomato plant survived in its Styrofoam cup. It was the inspiration for an entire vegetable garden for the storm victim. Planting a garden was more than hard work and a nice gesture. It was a first step towards recovery and taking control of the land. The potted tomato plant from the Styrofoam cup was the garden's centerpiece. There was hope for a harvest.

As for all the trees, I mourned their loss. Houses would be rebuilt and the land would eventually recover, but I wouldn't be on the planet when newly planted trees matured to the same heights as the old majestic hardwoods. The snags might serve as a lousy substitute, but the sight of them was a reminder of what was lost. And they were still ugly. I should have appreciated their usefulness because it wasn't long before even the snags were wiped clear away.

Shelly Van Meter Miller

27
MARCH MADNESS

TOR:CON 10. Rarely does the storm prediction center issue the highest number on the tornado Richter scale, but on March 2, 2012 they did. The last time the conditions were so favorable for a tornado outbreak was the epic day of April 27, 2011 when our worst weather nightmares came true. Less than a year later, Huntsville was not ready to rumble again. We were still reeling from the previous devastation and could not fathom another round of boxing with killer storms. However, another bout was about to begin. I could almost hear the bell ring, signaling the next round. I worried that our bell was about to be rung…again. Tornadoes were projected to touch down somewhere, but the real question was: where? Where was Jim Cantore from the Weather Channel? My brother joked, "What would you do if Jim Cantore showed up on your front doorstep?" Get the heck out of town! On March 2, 2012, Jim Cantore was in Louisville, KY, so we mistakenly believed that Alabama was in the clear.

I could not shake the feeling in the pit of my stomach that something catastrophic was about to happen. I could usually tell by my headache that a low pressure loomed, and yes, my head did hurt. The hairs on my arms bristled while I stood in the Publix parking lot, watching the bagger load groceries into my trunk. I examined my receipt to see how much I saved with coupons, but I anticipated a lightning strike any moment and eased my grip from the metal shopping cart, just in case. Lightning never came. Instead, the clouds harbored something more sinister.

Like déjà vu, the temperature hovered between 76-79 degrees while the unstable, humid air from the Gulf of Mexico rushed towards North Alabama. This was rocket fuel for the severe thunderstorm, Huntsville's main recipe ingredient. As I left the parking lot, the town of Killen, to the west of us, received softball-sized hail. It was only a matter of time. The time was 9:30 a.m. when the rain pounded my windshield before I could unload all the groceries. Outside the kitchen window, I saw our Leyland Cypress bushes swirling in circles, my unofficial indicator of wind circulation. When trees circulated, weather sirens weren't far behind. However, there weren't a lot of trees left after April 27th's tempests, so it was hard to tell.

Then came the predictable warning sirens. I hated knowing that a shelter was nearby but my children were not. My children were spread over three different schools and my husband worked on the third floor of his building. I could not drag the cat into the shelter with me while my loved ones could be exposed. Everyone knew to avoid driving during a warning, and I always wondered who would do such a thing. Then I knew. It was mothers trying to reach their children. At least one known casualty occurred from the '89 tornado on Airport Road while a mother was driving to her child's elementary school.

I wasn't the only mother who pulled up to the curb of the school while the siren pierced the air. The school discouraged parents from taking their children during an active warning, but had releases ready for our inevitable arrival, stating that the school was not responsible for any accidents once we signed the dotted line. Under the reason for check-out, I wrote, "TORNADO" in all caps. One mother asked if "tornado" was an excused absence, but no one answered her. At other schools, parents checked into the school and stayed with their children during the warning. Teachers found this helpful, with extra hands to help those children still traumatized from the last tornado tirade.

Meteorologists interrupted the regularly scheduled programs to list the already known areas of tornado destruction. The Limestone Penitentiary took a direct hit. We at first feared that inmates escaped instead of fearing that prisoners were hurt in the air raid. Not just any prison, Limestone was a maximum security prison for the most dangerous criminals. The prison housed 2100 criminals, 500 of them exposed to the fresh air when the penitentiary's roof peeled off and barbed wire security fence was tangled like spaghetti. The EF3 tornado assaulted the jail as it breached the metal bars and maximum security gates. But the tornado took no prisoners and all 2100 inmates survived and remained behind bars.

Schools released at 12:30 that afternoon, long enough to be counted as a school day. But this was too late for two North Alabama schools. Both Buckhorn High and Meridianville Middle schools were damaged by the same tornado that nearly freed the inmates at the penitentiary. Thankfully the tornado weakened by the time it reached the schools, but not before it devoured 45 homes in Limestone County and Harvest. The storm left 35,000 residents without power, some homes forever powerless in the ruins. The National Weather Service confirmed that as many as six tornadoes touched down in Madison County on March 2, 2012.

It seemed that poor Yarbrough Road was a roadway for tornadoes. Potholes still puckered the road from the April 2011 tornado assault. Researchers studied possible topographical data that would influence a tornado's touchdown, but so far they had no proven knowledge as to why tornadoes repeatedly visited the same areas, even the same streets. Their collective scientific answer was summed up in three words: "We don't know."

March's tornado did not wait for a scientific explanation to utilize the road as a thoroughfare again. Even amidst obvious signs that Yarbrough Road was still under construction, the twister did not reduce speed even while workers were present. Instead, it plowed through the reconstruction twice in ten months. Adding insult to injury, the new construction was toppled, and the temporary housing trailers were overturned as well. Not only did the tornado destroy the original home, it destroyed the temporary one, as well as the future home. The demolition was complete.

Trailers were discarded, homes were hollowed out, metal shrapnel was distorted, and muddy insulation covered the ground like old slush which northerners called, "Snirt." It was impossible to tell the current damage from the previous damage. Brand new roof shingles sparkled in heaps except for those hurled into the red mud, buried for good. Tornadoes visited Yarbrough Road so often that its property owners surveyed the damage and debris themselves and calculated, "That one was an EF3, not nearly as bad as the last one." The Enhanced Fujita scale rating would not label the tornado until months later, but Yarbrough Road residents were right on target. They knew the destructive effect of their tornadoes.

Forecasters called this tornado offensive, "March Madness." Born in Kentucky, I equated March madness with basketball championships. My first spelling words were h-o-r-s-e and p-i-g, thanks to granny shots and air balls while playing driveway basketball games. I would interpret a commentator's play-by-play of the March Madness tornado event like this: A tornado dribbled past the prison guards and took a shot at the Limestone Penitentiary. After a brief time-out, Harvest rebounded but another hook echo shot put the tornado in the lead again. The twister then committed three charging fouls against Yarbrough Road, as it tried to slam-dunk over two schools before fouling out.

Unlike Kentucky basketball, the March Madness tornado outbreak was not a game. Kentucky didn't come out on top, losing twenty-four lives during the torrential tornadoes. Huntsville did not lose any lives that day, but that did not mean that homes weren't ransacked or lives hijacked. We were sick and tired of playing tornado roulette. March Madness was a fitting description because we were in fact, mad.

We weren't sure how to deal with our madness, so we avoided making hard decisions and only dealt with things within our control. We spent most of the day in and out of tornado shelters and the rest of the afternoon looked like more of the same. Rinse and repeat. When there was a break between warnings, citizens took to the streets and came out of their hiding places to attempt normalcy. We all decided to run errands at the same time.

The corner drugstore was packed with people who had spent the day in solitary confinement in closets, bathrooms, or basements. We waited in long lines for necessities we would need in case we experienced another power outage. Some bought a carton of cigarettes while toilet paper was dangerously low on the shelves. A lady ahead in the line turned and I recognized a good friend. I purposely hid my purchase of hair coloring shampoo and cursed the tornadoes for giving me gray hair. I couldn't change the tornadoes, but I could change my hair. Just like jumping in and out of tornado shelters all day, I had to rinse and repeat. "Are you stocking up on supplies too?" I asked my friend.

"Oh no, my daughter is on the emergency response team and she just started her period. I've got to run this box of tampons to the tornado site so she can do her job," she answered. The men in line parted like the Red Sea at the mention of a menstrual cycle. In the South, March Madness took all forms, including funnel clouds and doting mothers. We controlled what we could and were powerless against nature's cycles and nature's fury.

Shelly Van Meter Miller

28
BLESS THIS MESS

What a mess! After four solid hours of sifting through sopping wet insulation, gathering crumbled drywall before it turned to mush in our fingertips, and heaving roof shingle after shingle atop a wobbly wheelbarrow, I was weary after the millionth load. If we had lined up all those stray roof shingles end to end, I am sure we could have roofed homes from Alabama to Alaska. I had never seen so many shingles, and each one was beginning to weigh as much as a lead blanket.

After the recent March Madness tornadoes, the well-worn path of each debris load created a muddy rut through the newly laid Bermuda sod. The wheelbarrows were piled high with wooden planks, laid across and balanced like see-saws. We would push off through the slimy grass with our hands on the wooden handles, but the load wouldn't budge until someone pushed us from behind and created momentum. Once the wheelbarrow overcame the inertia, there was hardly any stopping it. I almost flipped into the mile high pile in the sky of debris more than once. To say that I was tired was an understatement. I was plum-tuckered out tired, the kind of tired where you leaned against something just to hold you up, even if it was the port-a-potty next to you. The shady spots next to the industrial dumpster were already taken by other weathered volunteers of the tornado recovery.

The good thing about working yourself to death was that you rarely had time to think. If I stopped to ponder the magnitude of the tornado devastation, I would have to wring my hands, not knowing where to begin. One volunteer did this. He opened a folding chair and sat down on it, right in the middle of the mess. "I'm going home and getting rid of all my stuff," he said. Sifting through destroyed "stuff" could do that to you. How many plastic drinking tumblers or saved honey bear jars did a person need?

If I thought about how badly my heart ached for the storm victims, I would be good for nothing. It was better to keep moving. However, every victim that I met during the clean-up actually brightened my day. It made me wonder if I would hold up as well as they did, had it been my house that was plundered.

It felt good to take a break from the labor. By the looks of the debris pile, we had made some progress. Then again, the clean-up work yet to be completed was insurmountable. The neighborhood was crawling with relief workers, all busy as bees, but the work would not end today, or tomorrow, or the next day. I was not even sure that an end was in sight since I couldn't see past the mountain of debris. I worked alongside other volunteers who escaped the recent March Madness tornado wrath but were still cleaning up their own tornado mess from last April. The local high school students toiled along with us, giving up their Saturday to haul away the indiscernible wreckage, and looked as tired as we older folks did. I vowed to stop saying that teenagers were afraid of manual labor; they worked as hard as we did. Maybe they just needed to have a good reason. Two tornadoes striking the same area twice was reason enough.

A brave driver in a pick-up truck pulled up to the curb during our break. I wondered how many nails he would pluck out of his tires before circling the block. He offered us day-old bread and several stale, Valentine's Day boxes of chocolates. It was March but the timeworn chocolates were delightful. It was amazing how good the outdated food tasted. I didn't even bother to poke my fingernail in each piece of chocolate for early detection of coconut. I chewed the pieces in-between my coughing fits. "Sounds like you have the insulation cough," one of the workers commented. We all should have been wearing masks for the hazardous clean-up.

After my body cried, "Uncle!" one too many times, I gave in and gathered my crew to go home. I knew that there would be payback for working my body this hard. We peeled off our nasty work gloves that were bought specifically for this occasion, and almost tossed them into the debris pile too. We had crawled into mucky ditches, inhaled insulation particles, and probably lifted more weights than a bodybuilder on steroids could lift. I didn't even count the emotional toll from our labor. We struggled to handle broken dolls delicately in case they were still someone's beloved treasure, and didn't know what to do with the headless Wise Men from the Nativity set. Too many decisions on what to keep and what had to go. None of it was ours, yet the tough choices were ours.

We still had to retrieve our car that was across the busy road, parked at the church. The closer neighborhood streets were not navigable due to the debris strewn everywhere. We walked past homes spray painted with various FEMA markings on the bricks. Other homes were deserted, suggesting that nothing of value was left since no one was around to protect it. The church seemed many miles away and my legs struggled with every step, feeling as if my tennis shoes had been bronzed. I saw the crooked church steeple up ahead and the signature blue roof tarp waving in the breeze. The tornado had made a beeline for the church's sanctuary.

The skyline of broken rooftops was dotted with more blue tarps. The tarps made me think of a picture I had seen of a New Orleans couple in the wake of Hurricane Katrina. The couple made capes from the roof tarps and wrapped themselves with them while holding a sign: "FEMA came to town and all we got were these lousy blue tarps." I chuckled, in my delirium from overwork. The picture was a joke, but I hoped my town with their blue-tarped roofs would not be subjected to the same fate.

We trudged through the tall weeds snaking around our pant legs while we hugged the narrow shoulder of the road. If we didn't keep our eyes down on the asphalt, we could accidentally step out into the oncoming traffic. As cars whizzed past, my hair slapped across my face like steamers on a wind sock. I felt the warm exhaust from the cars and the heated stares from its occupants. We were a sight for sore eyes in our mud spattered jeans, sunscreen caked on our faces, and a farmer's tan on our forearms. It was possible that some people mistook us for a prison chain gang since we were close to the Limestone maximum security prison. Signs were posted periodically: Do not pick up hitchhikers. I imagined that I heard the clicks of car locks as the traffic passed by. Fellow citizens should know what tornado relief workers look like, although we did share a startling resemblance to prisoners on work release.

Finally back at the church parking lot, an aroma of charcoal filled the air. Ahead, a gathering of people turned to stare at us then quickly minded their stations. The church volunteers stood behind long cafeteria tables, donned their plastic gloves, and put on happy faces. They were volunteers happily serving other volunteers. A cleaning station was handy with anti-bacterial soap and wipes. Someone poured Milo's iced tea for me while someone else placed in my hand a piping hot hotdog in a fresh bun smothered with ketchup and mustard. I quickly forgot that I had just eaten a box of not-so-fresh chocolates. The hotdog was like pure manna from heaven. The food servers were congregation members of the same church whose blue roof tarp was waving in the wind. I commented that tornadoes sure did pick on churches. One of the church ladies replied, "We're so blessed."

I started, "Yeah, but…"

She interrupted me, "Watch out, now. We are blessed, indeed." And indeed they were. I was not about to argue. It was amazing how many people in Alabama believed that they were blessed to be hit by a tornado. They saw themselves as victors instead of victims.

The obvious blessing was making it through a tornado alive. Many miracles were documented during the 2011 tornado spree in Alabama. My favorite one concerned a family living in a mobile home in Harvest, AL. That April day, the family chose to "wait and see." They waited too long and then they really did see. They saw a twister funneling toward their trailer! They huddled together inside their trailer and prepared for flight.

The family of three latched arms and prayed while the oncoming tempest tore through their front door. Eyes were closed, hearts lifted to God, and the family swayed back and forth through the wind motion. When they opened their eyes, the family was still clutching one another but felt an extra pair of eyes watching them. A man was staring out his window to watch the tornado pass. Unbelievably, a family of three was dropped onto his front porch as the storm raged. The huddled group appeared to have fallen out of the sky and landed on his front porch. They were distant neighbors and they had never met. Neither he nor they would forget the day that a miracle dropped the tightly-knit family from the sky, along with an EF4 tornado. The family was treated for minor scratches, but their mobile home didn't sway as well as they did and was blown into oblivion. The family that prayed together stayed together.

Another person living in the same neighborhood slept soundly in his trailer during the raging storm. My bet was that he was a teenager. He was thrown out of bed when the twister knocked him to the floor to wake him up. The other half of his trailer looked like a train wreck, but the fellow was merely rudely awakened, another miracle.

While shopping for groceries, I met an employee whose house I knew had been swept away by the April 27th tornado spree. Over a year had passed, so I felt it was a safe question to ask how his rebuilding was progressing. I wasn't prepared for his answer. He replied that he was "blessed," but no, he wasn't back in his home yet. I found it odd since most victims were starting to get back on their feet with the reconstruction. He again mentioned that he was "blessed" to be able to rebuild so quickly, but another tornado blew his home away again. This kind man felt blessed even when hit twice by two tornadoes on separate occasions within the same year--talk about turning the other cheek.

Initially, he was the first to rebuild in his neighborhood after the tornado vacated his property. His reconstructed home was completed just in time for another tornado to blow it apart in March. National news reporters cornered him while seeking a story about tornado victims hit with double the trouble, two different tornadoes. As he surveyed his destroyed property with mud splattered on his face and sweat pouring down his back, he politely declined an interview despite the cameras in his face.

That day, he did Alabama a favor by not losing control on national TV. The media implied insult by asking, "Why would you rebuild on land cursed by continuous tornadoes?" New Orleans residents were asked the same question in the wake of Hurricane Katrina. Reporters insinuated that the hurricane's destruction was somehow their fault for living in a town below sea level. I saw the pain on my friend's face when faced with a similar question and its implications. It was his home. He had every right to rebuild.

He missed his home, but more specifically, he missed "the sound of his home." I never considered how a home sounded. Before his house reconstruction was completed this second round, he carted a plastic chair in his car trunk to sit in his empty yard. There were no trees anymore, nor were there neighbors. He just sat and listened to the comfort sounds of home. Then he would repack his folded chair and drive back to his temporary housing with the sounds of rushing traffic, banging from above, and strangers too close for comfort. He needed a regular dose of home sounds to get him through his current lease.

We discussed decorating ideas and paint color choices for his new home. During the first rebuilding, he chose a greenish tint for the walls called, "Tornado Watch." All traces of the fresh paint were gone now. He still felt blessed but wouldn't choose that color of paint again. He was tired of staring at the same green color on the inside walls, especially when it matched the tornado wall cloud on the outside. We were still chatting when my friend's name was called over the grocery store speaker to help the other cashiers. As he walked away to tend to his customers, he told me, "God Bless you."

When the devastating tornadoes shaved a razor-burn path through Alabama, the blackened stubble was all that was left. Storm victims had watched their possessions spinning around and then never saw them again. Many were homeless with all their belongings gone. Homeowners initially felt too blessed to be stressed because they lived through it. But after six months of displacement in a hotel, room service lost its appeal and the gloom of losing their home became reality. They just wanted "to go home." The long labor of love in homemaking went down the tornado drain. Property that had been in the family for generations was gone. To start over was overwhelming, especially as others second-guessed the victims' decisions, "Do you really want to rebuild there?" they judged.

Another tornado victim missed her "stuff," that she saw for the last time in April 2011. She rebuilt her home and finally had those granite countertops she had envied, and replaced her odds-n-ends furniture with the finest of pieces. When I asked her what she missed the most, she paused while my pen was poised for her response. She fought back tears, then barely audible, "Home. I just miss my home." She felt like a guest in her newly renovated home. Her property would not be recognizable on Google Earth satellite pictures either. As far as she was concerned, her home was still missing. Her response made me think of Dorothy from The *Wizard of Oz*. Dorothy knew what she was talking about when she said, "There's no place like home." She too had been through a tornado.

29
TORNADO ANNIVERSARY

Gardening is America's favorite pastime. Gardeners boast a huge affinity group, almost as large as Harley Davidson riders, and maybe even as popular as the trucking group. I belong to an elite gardening group, the lawn mower riders. I have my own Garden of Eden and love to get my hands dirty. One afternoon when all good gardeners should have been gardening, I chose not to kill my plants with kindness and took a break from the flower beds. I chose instead to watch my daughter compete in a track meet. I wish that I had recalled the story of what happened when Adam and Eve took a break from their garden.

As the gun lifted in the air, a loud "pop!" heralded the start of the 300 meter hurdle race, the most grueling of races as competitors ran the distance of the track while leaping over obstacles. I beat my palms against the chain link fence that separated me from the track. I felt as if I was at the Kentucky Derby except that I wore a hooded windbreaker instead of a derby hat and fancy dress, drank Gatorade instead of a mint julep, and it was my daughter running the race instead of a thoroughbred.

"C'mon, Girl!" I willed her to overtake her challenger. "You've got her now!" My heart raced as if I was the one running. My girl flew over the hurdles like a hovercraft and the best part of her race was about to begin—the end. This was her specialty, on the hunt for her opponent like a cheetah stalking a gazelle, and I already knew who would win as I watched from a safe distance. Her confidence passed through me as she shortened the breach and I heard the spikes on her cleats digging into the track. Both of us could taste the victory.

Suddenly, something went wrong. The wind stung her eyes and my daughter wiped her brow, and then wiped out. She flipped over the hurdle face first instead of feet first. She skidded on the surface and I instinctively turned away because it hurt to look. It was the type of scene that made a mother close her eyes and shake her head back and forth like an Etch-a-Sketch trying to erase the vision. I flinched as if I felt the burn of the asphalt too. I imagined the metallic taste of blood in the back of my throat. My husband was the closest to the finish line and hollered for someone to call for an ambulance. Suddenly everything moved in slow, blurred motion as if we were underwater. Then I saw it, a bone swimming in blood, in the place of where my daughter's finger used to be. In retrospect, I would have gladly chosen my flower bed over the hospital bed and a green thumb over my daughter's broken one. My dirty hands would have been better than my daughter's bloody hands.

When I heard the ambulance wail, I trembled and struggled to hold myself together. I raced to the passenger side of the ambulance but the driver apologized that it was against policy for a family member to ride in the ambulance if the child was over age fourteen. I slid the seatbelt across my lap and stared stonily at the dashboard. I was the one paying for the ride. I mumbled, "Let me out before the hospital if you'll get in trouble." The driver shrugged his shoulders and revved the ambulance engine to life. He explained that I could thank Hillary Clinton's legislation for forbidding mamas to ride in ambulances.

The ride would be shorter since the new Madison Hospital was now open for business. But the driver missed the turn on the road that was a straight shot to the emergency room. "Shouldn't you have turned there?" I pounced. The words were out of my mouth before I could retrieve them. I winced when I realized that I could have been the first person ever to get thrown out of an ambulance. The driver explained that a concerned citizen contacted the hospital board, complaining that emergency vehicles sped down his road. He suggested rerouting them unless it was a life or death situation. Between the concerned Madison citizen and Hillary Clinton, I thought we would never get to the new accommodating hospital.

Surgery was required to repair my daughter's finger. I pulled a nurse aside to ask whether we had competent hand surgeons in the area. She reassured me, "Honey, my son accidentally blew his finger off with a shotgun and the doctor sewed it back on so that you can't even tell now." I later found that Huntsville had one of the top hand surgeons in the Southeast, perhaps because we cling to our guns too much.

My daughter's operation was scheduled the next day, April 27, 2012. I would be at Huntsville Hospital on the anniversary of Alabama's worst weather tragedy, and in the exact same place I was during the tragedy the year before. Déjà vu was rarely a good memory, and this one wasn't either. I felt the tension and strain all week, leading up to the Day of Devastation anniversary. Everyone wanted the fateful anniversary date to hurry and pass. Unfortunately, members of my family were admitted to the hospital on both the Day of Devastation and the anniversary date, but fortunately they were both discharged with no life-threatening issues.

After my daughter's successful surgery, I administered a potent pain pill to her and promised to return to her bedside after transporting her sister to another track meet. I wheeled out of the driveway, paying no attention to the speed limits until I saw the flashing blue lights in my rear-view mirror. I pulled over to the side of Hughes Road, no longer amused by the "Hugs Road," nickname. It was lunch hour and every driver gawked at the person being pulled over by a policeman. Even worse, I pretended that the policeman was after someone else and that I was just being courteous by pulling aside for him to pass. I wondered if that trick ever worked for anyone because it didn't for me. The officer pulled directly behind my car, signaling that I was the blue light special.

I fumbled in the console for my insurance card and felt the stares of everyone on Hughes Road. Mortified, I felt my body violently shaking and realized that I was "losing it." The officer noticed my shaking too and backed off while his hand slid to his revolver. I only cried harder when I realized that my crying fit caused him to think that I was a deranged and dangerous criminal. He asked if I was okay (from a safe distance) and I hiccupped, "I am not okay! My daughter is drugged up!" His hand touched his gun again.

After spilling my saga, the understanding policeman showed leniency and issued me a traffic warning. I read it through my tears and saw that it was dated April 27th. Had it been any other day, I would have spent the next month in traffic school. The dated warning in my hand reminded me of my humiliation over being pulled over, but I had a feeling that very few tickets were going to be issued that day.

I had built up the anniversary date beforehand in my mind, preparing for a difficult one. Everyone had an unspoken understanding and extended grace to one another on that day. The first anniversary after the devastating storms was full of emotion as we all dreaded its approach. It was worse for some than it was for others, but the date passed and we made it through another day. I really missed my garden.

30
LOST AND FOUND

I used to wear socks with holes in them. My mother would chastise me, "Wouldn't you be embarrassed if you had to go to the emergency room?" I assured my mother that I would have more to worry about than my socks if I had to go to the emergency room. There were worse things to be caught with other than holey socks. For instance, one Huntsville man found himself in a compromising situation when the 1989 tornado struck. I tried to put myself in his shoes, but he wasn't wearing any. In fact, he was barely wearing anything.

A driver sat in his car, stalled in traffic while trying to get home. The tornado had just plowed through Airport Road only moments before. Someone knocked on his car window while he waited. The stranger wanted to hitch a ride, but he noticed the stranger was only wearing underwear. Under any other circumstances, the driver would have fled and left his car with the naked man. However the self-conscious man in underwear begged the driver for clothing, not for his car. The story was even stranger than the stranger. The naked man lived in a second-story apartment on Airport Road and was actually in his bathroom when the tornado struck. When he opened his eyes, he was hugging the toilet bowl, and in the apartment below him. The man was able to walk away, although not far without any clothing.

The tornado tales go back as far as 1974. I just heard a new one last week. An artist at a craft show remembered the '74 tornado when she was a young girl. After the funnel cloud touched down, she found an airplane wing in her backyard. She'll never forget that image for the rest of her life. Her neighbor found a paper document from Canada. The 1974 Super Tornado outbreak did include a tornado in Canada that same day, apparently carrying debris all the way to Alabama.

Sometimes the stories were the same, but with a different twist. Some sagas were so outrageous that they had to be true. No one could make this stuff up. Everyone had a tornado story, whether it was theirs, their friend's, or a friend of a friend's. Tornado experiences in the Valley were something that everyone talked about while waiting in doctor's offices and in grocery lines. Storm experiences in the Valley were both prevalent and personal. No one was left untouched.

When tornado talk arose, it seemed that every person within a group would relay a tornado account that she knew to be true. I dreaded these chance meetings because usually someone in the group would be especially silent. Either their tornado tale was too fresh or too painfully personal. Everyone had a story to tell. It was when you least expected it, that the one quiet person admitted, "My grandmother died in that tornado." Everyone would pause awkwardly, wanting someone else to break the delicate silence.

We characterized a tornado as a freak of nature, and the more freakish, the more interesting the story. The story took a different twist when the tornado crossed paths with someone we loved. Sometimes we glorified the tornadoes and were distressed to witness someone else's tragic tornado experience. But no matter where you stood on the tornado spectrum, one thing was certain: You had to talk about it. Even the folks that were still in the throes of reconstruction wanted to talk about it. Those still grieving over lost ones didn't want their loved ones forgotten either. I came to the conclusion that the only way to get past the terror of it all was to talk it to death, or even better, to listen.

We still talked about what we lost on the April Day of Devastation. Every time that a fallen tree was mentioned, it prompted a tornado discussion. If you still had trees, they displayed a nice show of fall color in November. We were surprised to have a fall at all due to the summer drought. Alabama's climate usually changed from hot to cold, forcing all the leaves to fall and change colors while on the ground. The hot-to-cold shock was one of the reasons that tornadoes came to visit as often as they did. November was a time to remember as we entered our second tornado season of the year. Meteorologist Bob Henson told *Our Amazing Planet* that so far, 2012 was the least active tornado year on record for the United States. That was something to be thankful for before Thanksgiving.

The season reminded us to count our blessings. Along with the blessings we had, we also couldn't forget what we lost, because sometimes you didn't know what you had until you lost it. We lost a great deal on April 27, 2011 and we knew it. Besides the obvious loss of property and devastated land, Alabama lost what neither time nor money could replace. It wasn't just objects and stuff that we lost, but more importantly, it was what they represented. One friend lost a canoe, not just any canoe though. Her canoe was her first major purchase when graduating from college. Most students saved to afford a new car, but my friend chose to save for a canoe. After buying the boat, she asked a certain fellow to go canoeing with her.

"Sure, who else is going?" he asked.

"Just you," she answered, slightly embarrassed.

This was how she propositioned her future husband for a first date. They canoed that day and continued to canoe twenty years later on their private lake. The canoe was a symbol of the beginning of their life together. On April 27th, the tornado thrust the canoe into a tree and wrapped it around a tree's trunk like a taco shell. The strange sight didn't hurt as much as seeing the canoe grabbed by the crane's teeth and crushed into scrap metal afterwards. When the deformed piece was heaped onto the junk pile with the rest of the garbage, my friend felt the loss.

April 27th, 2011 not only stole first date memories, but for Pastor David, a twentieth wedding anniversary celebration. He had planned a dinner for his wife and him that Wednesday evening to celebrate two decades of marriage. His ambitious plans disintegrated early that morning, the minute he opened the church doors as a shelter for the upcoming storms. It was after midnight that he finally remembered that his twentieth anniversary came and went. On his anniversary celebration evening, he shared fast food with strangers and slept on a cot next to six men that he didn't know. His town of Harvest would remember the anniversary day, but not in a good way.

Other celebrations were expected to take place on April 27th as well. When a volunteer clean-up crew sifted through one tornado site, one of the crew members came upon a nice dish that was not shattered like the rest. She uncovered the debris from the top of the dish and dusted off the cloth napkin that lay on top. Underneath, she found a pyramid of tiered crab cakes, ready to be served. The home's interior was turned upside-down, but the crab cake appetizers were perfectly aligned. What was even stranger, the crab cakes didn't belong to the occupants of the house, nor any of their close neighbors. A birthday party down the road lost their crab cakes and didn't know where to find them.

Some lost their birthday celebrations. My pastor's wife missed her own April 27th birthday. She missed the surprise party that never happened. Church members had planned to surprise her with cake that evening during church service. Had she shown up as planned, she would've been met by a dark church with locked doors. Only those seeking asylum from the storm were sheltered in the church basement, and we weren't having a party. We would remember her "half-birthday" six months later. There was actually a lost birthday celebration club formed in Alabama for people such as my pastor's wife.

Several high schools cancelled their proms. As a mother of girls, I knew the fanfare involved in getting a Southern belle out the door on prom night. The "Is he going to ask me, or not?" issue consumed the month of April. It then spiraled uncontrollably into the hair, the make-up, the nail appointment. Then the matching corsage, dinner reservations, costly tickets, and prom decorations were nailed down. Finally, the most important thing was not the date, but the dress. Most girls had the dress before they had the date. The Saturday after the April storm was a popular prom night for many high schools. Some seniors missed their first and only prom when power failure canceled their major event. Perhaps they could have a prom as one of their class reunions. But it wouldn't be the same because again, it was all about the dress.

College seniors missed their graduation ceremonies. Universities across northern Alabama not only canceled final exams and classes for the semester, they also postponed graduation ceremonies. College graduates would not receive their diploma until the following August. A delayed degree interfered with many post-graduate plans. A late graduation and no diploma in hand possibly cost college graduates missed job opportunities. Careers could have been delayed because of the tornado outbreak.

Instead of losing something that couldn't be replaced, one friend told of what she found after the tornado. She was out of town during the twister rampage, but came back to her Madison home after the power outage was over. Her home appeared untouched after the storms, but upon inspecting her screened porch, she found a letter waiting for her. The storm blew the letter under her storm door. Although it may have been meant for her, the letter wasn't addressed to her.

The letter was from a country club in Phil Campbell, AL, addressed to one of its members. After the April 27th EF5 tornado obliterated Hackleburg, the next town in the line of destruction was Phil Campbell. The same tornado travelled almost one hundred miles on the ground, carrying much of Phil Campbell with it, on its way to Tennessee. The violent EF5 dispersed items and letters like a ticker tape parade, raining down on every town in-between. While Madison was not one of the towns in the tornado's path, there was no rhyme or reason for how Mother Nature distributed the debris.

In finding a lost letter, my friend gained an added burden. She checked online and found that the person to whom the letter was addressed was deceased. The tornado not only took the letter, but also took the addressee's life. My friend planned to drive to Phil Campbell that next weekend, not only to return the letter, but to offer her help and sympathy for the small town. After all, she felt that God sent her the letter, asking for help.

The lost letter reminded us of losses that we didn't like to talk about. Last week was the first time that I met someone who lost a family member in the April 27th tornadoes. A memorial was dedicated in nearby Limestone County for all those who perished and honored the rescue workers who were the first responders to the aftermath. Bricks from victim's destroyed homes were used for the monument. Family members gathered and comforted one another while staring at the names of their loved ones etched in stone. Some family members wore matching t-shirts with their lost loved one's picture printed on the front, and an angel and Bible verse on the back of the shirt. When I asked about the Bible verse, that was when I learned about Gilwood Park.

Shelly Van Meter Miller

31
GILWOOD PARK

"What's your name, Sweetheart?" the Vacation Bible School leader asked the child.

"Shannon Gail Rudd," the fast-talking child replied.

"Tell me again and please slow down this time, Honey." When the leader asked Shannon to slow down her speech, it sounded to Shannon as if she had said, "Su-lo day-own," with a slow Southern drawl. Shannon could never speak that slowly if she tried and repeated her name again, "Shannon Gail Rudd," this time louder but still in one swift breath. The VBS leader printed Shannon's name as it sounded to her. Shannon's Bible school certificate was made out to: Shannon "Gilwood." The name stuck and Shannon was nicknamed "Gilwood" until she turned forty.

Around her fortieth birthday, Shannon wrote a letter to her mother. In the letter Shannon quoted a Bible verse from Jeremiah 29:11: For I know the plans I have for you," declares the Lord, "plans to prosper you and not to harm you...".-(NIV) Shannon told her mother that she felt as if God was speaking directly to her with this verse. Her mother cherished the letter but was devastated two months later when Shannon was killed on April 27, 2011, a victim of the tornado that struck Limestone County near Huntsville. Her mother's home in Madison, AL had been struck by a different tornado earlier that day. Because of the timing of the Madison morning tornado that struck her mother's home, family members were able to see Shannon one last time before a more violent tornado would take her life that same afternoon.

Shannon was there for her parents when their home and two cars were damaged by the 11:00 a.m. tornado. "Don't worry, we'll clean this up. People will help us," Shannon consoled her parents. She hauled away debris for most of the day, piling it on the adjacent property's swampland. By late afternoon, the weather threatened again. Shannon grabbed Bubba, her dog, and drove to Limestone County to check on her grandmother. Witnesses saw Shannon cradling her dog when she approached her grandmother's front porch at 4:30 p.m. She reached for the front door as the house exploded. An EF-5 tornado ripped through the house and unleashed at the exact time of Shannon's arrival.

The tornado was so strong that it crumbled the home's foundation and the rest of the house and porch disappeared. Bubba made it through the storm. Shannon did not. Shannon's grandmother was injured when thrown from the home and crawled to Shannon's jeep that weathered the twister. Until she saw the jeep, the grandmother was unaware that Shannon was ever in harm's way. A neighbor rescued the grandmother and used a door as a stretcher to carry her to a nearby undamaged home where all the injured lay in triage. There, rescue workers performed so much more than first aid.

Shannon was not only a granddaughter and a daughter; she was also a mother who left three children behind. Had Shannon survived the tornado, she would have met her new baby granddaughter and become a grandmother, herself. Her sad story would end as another tragic outcome from the Day of Devastation. Following the tornado attacks, there were so many similar heartbreaking stories of lives cut short, being in the wrong place at the wrong time, and loved ones not getting to say their final goodbyes, but Shannon's story would not end there.

One year later, a park was dedicated and named for Shannon's Vacation Bible School nickname, "Gilwood." Gilwood Park was built as a memorial for all of the area's tornado victims who lost their lives on that fateful Wednesday in April. The community park is located next to Shannon's parents' home, on the former swampland next door to their property. Gilwood Park was built almost entirely with donated materials. If it was made of wood, Home Depot donated it. Woodmen of the World and other charity groups donated or discounted material for the park's completion.

Gilwood Park is a peaceful refuge with flowers, benches, bridges and birdbaths. A chapel was the first structure built, and angels abound in the park in the form of statues and stepping stones. A covered pavilion with a stone fireplace welcomes guests most any time of the year. A dog-bone shaped garden brings a smile to visitors, as well as the larger-than-life giraffe that can be seen from Wall Triana Highway. University of Alabama fans would be happy to know that their mascot, a giant elephant, also resides in the park as one of the favorite pieces of playground equipment. The playground animals make the park a popular destination for toddler playgroups and family reunions. Gilwood Park was constructed for those seeking peace and quiet, memorable times with friends, or recreational family get-togethers. The newest addition to the park is a train with six cars. Children can ride around the park with plenty to entertain them while the adults enjoy a peaceful visit. It truly is a park for all ages.

Perhaps the most significant addition to Gilwood Park is an underground tornado shelter for the community that was donated by Durable Designs. Painted like a giant ladybug so that children would not be afraid, the shelter is visible from the park's entrance and can hold up to 40 occupants. Children enjoy using the certified FEMA shelter door as a sliding board. For now, the giant ladybug tornado shelter is used for their entertainment, but in the future it may be used to save their lives. Gilwood Park was built with the future in mind—Shannon's legacy. The rest of Shannon's favorite Bible verse, Jeremiah 29:11, states: For I know the plans I have for you," declares the Lord, "plans to prosper you and not to harm you, plans to give you hope and a future."- (NIV) Hope is alive in Gilwood Park. As for the future, I like the way Mahatma Gandhi put it: "The future depends on what you do today."

https://www.facebook.com/GilwoodPark

Shelly Van Meter Miller

32
LIFE'S A BEACH

Ain't life a beach? It was in North Alabama although the nearest natural beach is over 300 miles away on the Gulf of Mexico. I kept a yearly vigil over the Gulf waters, staring at the sugar sand and pristine beach from my sunken beach chair. We frequented the same Gulf Shores year after year, but my, how the beach had changed! Or maybe it was me that changed.

Oh sun, please stay behind those pearly clouds, I now begged. As a teenager, I craved ultra-violet rays and wished for the sun to beam me up with its warm solar power. I slathered Hawaiian Tropic oil over my slender body and shook the beads in my Bo Derek braided hair-do while strutting in my string bikini along the Gulf Coast beaches, lovingly called "Redneck Riviera" by locals. My mom would not have approved. This I knew because my younger brother idolized Farrah Fawcett Majors and longed for a belt buckle with Farrah's swimsuit calendar photo as its centerpiece. Mom sidestepped the belt buckle issue since Farrah's photo at the time was deemed inappropriate. She suggested they shop for a buckle in which the Farrah image wasn't wearing a swimsuit. "You mean they sell those?" my brother gasped excitedly. If Farrah's one-piece suit was unsuitable, I knew mine would be. So I slipped into the nearest beach hotel and changed like Houdini from my modest Speedo swimsuit that Mom picked out, into my itsy bitsy teeny weeny bikini that I picked out.

And then I got married and had kids. The bikini dilemma was no longer an issue. No longer winding our cooler trails across the sandy beach, we instead dragged pack-and-play baby beds through sand drifts with high hopes that baby would nap and not eat the sandy beach. Babies grew into young children and we continued to frequent the Gulf beaches and often bring along guests.

Several years later we hosted one of the Children of Chernobyl, a mission for Russian children whose families were affected by Russia's Chernobyl Nuclear Plant explosion in 1986. Our host child only spoke Russian and we only spoke English, which made life much more interesting. But our Russian guest, Maryna, was very teachable. When we planned a beach trip, I prepared Maryna with magazine pictures of the sun and surf since she had never seen the ocean before. I taught her to say the word, "beach." Maryna was slowly learning English vocabulary and fondly called me, "Mama Shelly." But with a Russian accent, the vowel sounds were weaker, so when she said, "beach," it sounded like "bich." We worked daily on the long "ea" vowel sound, but every time she pointed to the calendar to countdown for the beach, she combined the only English words she knew to communicate, "Mama Shelly, bich?" She questioned me in this way until I thought the beach trip would never come. When it did, as soon as the white sand squished between Maryna's toes, she kicked up her heels, throwing sand in my face, and waved her hands excitedly toward the crashing waves. Everyone on the crowded shore turned to watch the spectacle and heard her shouting over the surf, "Mama Shelly, bich! Mama Shelly, bich!"

Yes, this was still the same beach, and I was now Mama Shelly, quite happy if the name stopped there. The beach brought many memories that would outlast the sand that lingered in my car from the trips. Thank goodness we were past the pet hermit crab phase. We accidentally killed so many pet hermit crabs that only one lived long enough to receive a name. The only reason Hermie lived longer was because my daughter had given him CPR. I couldn't believe it worked and thought the crab would never die.

Sitting under a beach umbrella, I wondered where to apply for a job as an 'umbrella guy.' The umbrella staff had it made in the shade. So many years had passed since my itsy bitsy teeny weeny bikini days. I now found myself wishing for additional sun block as I shielded myself from the sun's rays and wore a Speedo swimsuit for maximum coverage with a flowing skirt, no less. The sensuous suntan oil melted away like those teenage years. I caked on sunscreen like layers of icing and grabbed a floppy beach hat to shield my scalp from the blistering sun. I had changed, but the beach had not.

This was the same beach now tainted by the Deepwater Horizon's explosion, the accident that left flora and fauna covered in oil along the beaches of the Gulf of Mexico. Even now, the paid tar ball collectors rode the sand dunes in golf carts and sifted through my seashells with gloved hands. I bent down to touch a real tar ball from the oil spill and the hunter/gatherer protested, "Don't touch that!" as if it were uranium. He tried to save me from an oil stain.

Every beach cloud had a silver lining, literally. Now older, I saw the beach in a different light. The sunbeams penetrated the deep sea causing little diamonds to flash like strobe lights as the waves flickered past. The ebb and flow of the tides and nature's stunning beach displays were the highlights of my current beach trips. Its splendor was always there, but the beauty had often gone unnoticed by me. Youth was definitely wasted on the young.

Weather experts viewed the beach in a different light too. When asked why North Alabama had so many deadly tornadoes, meteorologists concurred and chimed the same three words: Gulf of Mexico. According to the *Southern Living Gardening Book*, "Nothing has a more profound effect on our region's climate and weather than the Gulf of Mexico." The tropical air from the Gulf marched north to battle Canadian air, creating a convergence zone. Our area was in the middle of this convergence zone.

My Alabama home reaped what the Gulf of Mexico sowed although 365 miles away. When we encountered the outer storm bands from hurricanes that came across Alabama, they maintained tropical storm status when they reached Huntsville. It felt like life was a beach in Alabama, except we were minus the waves, but as usual we had the wind. Our hot summer days were packed with what felt like a million degree humidity. This too was blamed on the Gulf of Mexico. Because of our city's placement on the map, Northern Alabama was a popular birthplace for tornadoes. According to city-data.com, Huntsville's tornado activity is higher than the state's average. In fact, Huntsville's tornado average is 266% higher than the overall United States average-- not a statistic that we would want to advertise on our visitor and tourism websites.

Alabama's tornado statistics were calculated before our April 27,

2011 tornado raid. The new percentage is certain to be staggering. Doyle Rice who covers weather for USA Today, notes that the most tornado damage overall from 1950-2011 has occurred in Texas and Alabama. Considering the size of Alabama vs. Texas, tornadoes are more concentrated in our state. The most damaging tornado month is April. In Huntsville, the most damaging tornado day is Wednesday, by my estimations. We would be better off spending every Wednesday in April in an underground bunker.

Perhaps we should warn potential new residents of Madison County about the likelihood of bad weather. Recently, new neighbors from out West moved to the end of our cul-de-sac. No sooner did the moving trucks leave when they returned several weeks later. The lady of the house complained that Alabama wasn't for her. In less than a month, a snake slithered into her yard and she suffered through two tornado drills. "Alabama gave me one last present as I was packing up the yard tools," she grumbled. She rolled up her sleeves to show me a bad case of poison ivy on her arms. The snake was harmless and the tornadoes didn't actually touch down. The poison ivy…well, that was bad. I felt sorry for her and was reminded of the time when spiders drove me out of the Midwest.

After the super cell tornadoes landed in our backyard on April 27, 2011, many of us fled the scene and migrated further south to the Gulf beaches. Our family did not seek greener pastures or whiter sand during the crisis. My dad instilled in me at a young age, "When the going gets tough, the tough get going." Some took the mantra literally and thought it meant to "get going" to the beach. But we stayed, stuck it out, and did not desert our town in its hour of need. The fact that we could only travel as far as our empty tank of gas could take us and that "we" had a kidney stone to pass factored in the decision.

Months after Huntsville's tornado havoc, we vacationed at the Gulf beaches again. A convenience store clerk asked the question of the day, "Where y'all from?" When we mentioned Huntsville, he replied, "I'm still praying for you, Huntsville."
"Thank you," I answered. Then I remembered my stroll down the beach earlier that morning while instead of dodging beached jellyfish, I sidestepped bleached tar balls. "I'm still praying for you too, Gulf Shores," I added.

33
THE REST OF THE STORY

Sharon-Harvest, AL

Exactly one month after the April 27, 2011 tornado, Sharon's home was declared unlivable. Sharon braced herself to watch the bulldozer shove her house remains to the end of the driveway. It had taken this long to prepare the land and home for its final blow. When she and her husband surveyed their property after the tornado, they made some unusual discoveries.

Water had been completely sucked out of the toilet bowl and oil was totally sucked out of their totaled car's engine. Their neighbor who rode out the storm in his basement, gasped for air while on the phone as the tornado sucked the breath out of him.

While the tornado swept most things away, it resurrected other things. Before Sharon and her husband built their home that was now a pile of debris, another home that was destroyed by a tornado during the 1974 Super Tornado Outbreak existed on the same property. For years they had searched for remnants of the other home but had been unable to locate where the former house once stood. After their April 27th tornado, another foundation appeared on the back of Sharon's property. The recent tornado resurrected the foundation from the previous house by pulverizing the land around it, causing its foundation to rise to the surface.

Soaked piles of insulation were removed from Sharon's home, but the insulation was not the same color. The insulation had come from someone else's home. A picture frame appeared undamaged, but in-between the frame and glass was a bit of the insulation, again the wrong color. Sharon tried to salvage a new couch, but as a volunteer swept the shards of glass from it, the broom kept snagging on the cushion. On closer observation, a fish hook was found embedded in the couch. Neither Sharon nor her husband enjoyed fishing, so someone in Alabama was missing his fishing tackle that had found its way into their couch cushion.

Whatever was salvageable had been loaded into a POD storage unit already. Sharon's husband located his new Bible in the ruins but it was dilapidated and torn to shreds. Still, he couldn't throw it away, so he just left it inside the wrecked house. The bulldozer plowed all of it under and pushed the massive pile on top of the dead tree limbs from Jamie's tree, the hardwood planted to commemorate her son's birth.

As tears streamed down Sharon's face, little things sparked hope for her. When volunteers had sifted through the storm-trashed debris, a potted Geranium plant had overturned in the storm and was headed to the ever-growing debris pile. Something green caught Sharon's eye first. It was a tiny maple seedling living in the same pot. The seedling must have come from one of the hundreds of helicopter seeds that drove her crazy this time of year—falling from Jamie's tree. Jamie was an adult now but Sharon pampered the maple tree seedling so that Jamie could plant it to commemorate his own son's birth, her grandson.

And as for the neighbor's dog which was blown out the back door and believed to be gone for good, he returned at 10:00 a.m. the morning after the tornado. The dog was unharmed but something was definitely different about him. He was no longer a hyper and unruly dog. Instead, he was almost clingy, laying his head on anyone's lap as if to communicate, "You have no idea what kind of night I had."

Laura-East Limestone, AL

After the April 27, 2011 tornadoes, Laura spent the next six months in a cramped hotel room with her family of four. She became a spokesperson for LawLer's Barbeque commercials because the pork platter special was the closest thing to a home-cooked meal that she had in half a year. Her home had $100K in foundation repairs and was undergoing reconstruction. The garage had separated from the rest of the house and the vertical crack that sliced the front of her home from top to bottom was a major issue.

Some days were better than others. At first Laura felt that tornado destruction was the norm and she took it all in stride. After all, she remembered that her Grandmother in Guinn, AL had gone through similar devastation in 1974 when Laura had visited her. Tornadoes must be a way of life for the people in Alabama, she figured. The thought of putting her house back together again made her miss her Iowa home that she left less than a year before.

It was at a baseball game that she got upset with her circumstances. While sitting on the bleachers, she listened to the other parents and fans discussing their lives and routines. They talked about their gardens, what they were going to fix for dinner, normal everyday stuff. It was the stuff they didn't talk about that enlightened her. They didn't mention insurance agents, FEMA, contractors, burn piles or hotel rooms. Laura felt very much alone and realized that tornado recovery was a lonely road. Although her feelings were normal, there was nothing normal about life following a tornado strike.

Laura was able to spend 2011's Thanksgiving in her newly reconstructed home. Only one of her neighbors chose to rebuild, so her house stood out in the barren field and was easily seen from the road. After the countless burn piles' embers smoldered, her land was clear of trees. Before the storm, she had nowhere to plant a garden due to the amount of shade in her yard. Since all shade disappeared when the last tree fell, the gardener in her began to make horticultural schemes. She had her refurbished basement home and now she could have a garden and maybe a horse. She had all kinds of plans for the land. It was now a clean slate.

Laurel (Down the street from Laura) – East Limestone

"Mom, where are you? I love you!" the text read. It was from Laurel's daughter on the night of April 27th, but Laurel didn't receive the text until a week later. Important communication was missed or disjointed during the tornado aftermath.

Laurel had so many things on her mind now. She remembers falling in love with their house the instant she saw it. It was everything she ever wanted in a home. So why now did she wish they would just condemn her house, demolish it, and start over? Because it would have been easier than watching her pride and joy gutted as contractors tried to make her home livable again.

She also had more important matters on her plate. When her dad collapsed on her garage steps the afternoon of the tornado, medical tests indicated that this was a sign of a more dangerous problem other than fatigue from running through the streets to check on his daughter's family. Since the April 27th tornadoes, Laurel's father underwent two open heart surgeries to repair damage. Both surgeries involved long recoveries, and those recoveries would take place while living in a rental home. Although her parents' home appeared intact when Laurel hurried to check immediately following the tornado, the house actually rotated several inches off its foundation and required extensive repair.

The tornado complicated Laurel's life in many ways. Everyone expected her to bounce back to her usual, bubbly and cheerful self. She wished she could be as carefree as Sammy. Sammy the horse was seen shortly after the tornado, munching hay nonchalantly, oblivious to the tree and neighborhood debris that surrounded him in the field. The tornado did not interfere with his "hay" day.

But life wasn't that simple. When the next tornado warning came along after the April 27th Day of Devastation, Laurel found herself at a frozen yogurt shop. A Bible study group sat next to her table on the shop's outside patio. As soon as the warning siren sounded, Laurel took precaution. She noticed that the study group looked toward the sky and then bowed their heads in prayer. Laurel was a praying woman too, but she could pray, eat yogurt, and get away from the storm at the same time. She could be bubbly again, but no, she could not ever be carefree during a tornado warning.

Shelly-Madison, AL

I could never be a storm chaser. I would always be the one that the storm chased. When I was young, I loved to play hide-n-seek. Nobody wanted to be "it" though because "it" was solo. To avoid being "it," we scrambled in a panic to find a good hiding place before whoever was "it" came after us. Some chose the exact hiding place again and again. I always wondered why they did that. Some players took so much time to find a place to hide that they weren't ready at all whenever "it" counted down from the number twenty. Time always ran out for them and "it" chased them first, allowing the rest of us to reach home base.

No matter how good my hiding place was, there was always one moment that my heart pounded hardest. It was the instant that "it" stopped counting for only a second's hesitation. The anticipation would make me gasp inward and hold my breath. I knew "it" was coming. Then "it" would startle the silence and yell, "Ready or not, here I come!" That was fun then, but I was too old for that now and didn't enjoy being chased.

When I saw my first wall cloud on April 27, 2011, I drove away from the potential tornado as if I was being chased. I didn't waste any time in transporting my family to the church basement for shelter. My children hung onto the hooks inside the car that were meant to hang pressed clothes from the cleaners. I swerved around the road curves so fast that we looked as if we were riding on a subway train with hands grasping the straps.

Once we were safe in the basement, we texted my brother in Kentucky and told him that we saw a tornado forming but were in a safe place. In his next text, my brother requested a picture, so we took a picture of our family in the church basement and emailed it. "I meant of the tornado," he texted back. There would be no tornado recordings from me, for I would not come out of my bunker until the coast was clear, or in this case, the sky. Besides, being technically challenged, the last time I attempted to take a video with my phone, the only footage I captured was several minutes of my own foot.

Within a week of the deadly April tornadoes, my life was back to normal. Those of us who were physically untouched by the storms weren't "home-free" though. We would be emotionally touched forever. I walked through too many condemned houses belonging to good friends. I sorted through their ruins and got sunburned while inside of their homes. Portions of roofs were missing, allowing the sun to bake those inside the home. Most of us neglected to apply sunscreen while indoors.

The clean-up assignment was run like an assembly line. Minor obstacles were removed so that we could be more efficient. A chandelier that barely hung from an exposed rafter kept making contact with volunteers' heads, so one man reached up with his cutter and severed the chord. The chandelier fell to the ground but no one cared. My husband stepped aside and I saw him remove a nail from the bottom of his shoe. He tossed the nail into the trash pile and kept working.

I watched as other workers moved furniture out of the house and walked through an open area that used to be the doorway. There was a more direct route to the dump now that the walls had fallen down, but as creatures of habit, they still used the doorway because that was what you were supposed to do when you entered someone else's house—walk through the front door. One lady even stopped to straighten a plaque that hung near the doorframe. The house was turned inside-out but it was bothersome to look at a crooked picture. I read the words on the plaque hanging sideways: Bless all who enter here.

I rummaged through all my friends' stuff, hoping to find something meaningful that they could take away from the storms. It was demeaning to ask whether each item was important to them, "Do you want this plastic NASCAR tumbler and what about these fake Easter eggs?" Or, "I put your socks in the same box as your dishes so that the plates wouldn't get broken while in storage."

One simple statement or item found could open up a can of wounds. After a certain amount of time, we expected tornado victims to "hurry up and get better." We didn't like to see their pain drawn out for months. Because we were anxious to move past the tragedy, we sometimes came across as impatient when victims weren't moving past their grief fast enough for us. These were uncomfortable times, but they also brought us closer together.

I appreciated those who shared their grief and losses with me in the writing of this story. At first I was afraid to hear their stories and timid to ask the hard questions, but would leave the interviews feeling inspired and uplifted. Yes, I even felt blessed. The tornadoes forged new friendships and we were all in this together.

We were not naïve enough to believe that the tornadoes were done infiltrating our lives. Since living in Huntsville's "Tornado Valley," I had seen a quarter of a century's worth of tornadoes. Nothing suggested that times would change. We would be the ones that would change or be changed.

It was our relationship with this land that made it special ..."for better, for worse, for richer, for poorer, in sickness and in health, to love and to cherish..." Huntsville would rise again, even when the countdown stopped. Over the years, we had seen our city survive, revive and even thrive. We built rockets that launched out of this world, so we could rebuild Huntsville from the ground up if we had to. After all, we were rocket scientists. Despite this Tornado Valley we lived in, we would overcome.

Ready or not, here "it" comes!

Shelly Van Meter Miller

SOURCES

Bender, Steve, ed. The Southern Living Garden Book. Oxmoor House, Inc., Copyright 1998, p. 36.

Bryant, Chris. "Tweets that Touched Lives." Find Your Passion. December 15, 2012 www.au.edu.

Causey, Donna. "Stars Fell on Alabama." Alabama Pioneers: The Alabama Genealogy Resource! December 15, 2012 www.alabamapioneers.com.

"Falling of the Stars." Patmos Papers. December 15, 2012 www.patmospapers.com/ndex/stars.htm.

"Famous Large Tornado Outbreaks in the United States." NOAA National Weather Service National Forecast Office: Milwaukee/Sullivan, WI. December 15, 2012 www.crh.noaa.gov/mkx/?n=torout.

"Field Operations Guide for National Urban Search and Rescue." Federal Emergency Management Agency. 2003. December 15, 2012 www.fema.gov

"Fujita Scale." Wikipedia. December 15, 2012 http://en.wikipedia.org/wiki/enhanced_fujitascale.

"Gilwood Park." Facebook. December 15, 2012 www.facebook.com/gilwoodpark

Hansen, Jeff. "April Tornadoes Legacy." The Birmingham News. 28 April 2012.

Interview with Bob Baron, December 2012

Main, Douglas. "2012 Could Break Record for Fewest Tornadoes." Our Amazing Planet. November 20, 2012. December 15, 2012 www.ouramazingplanet.com.

Marshall, Mike. "At Harvest Church, it has been "an amazing week, and, oh my goodness, the stories." The Huntsville Times. 02 May 2011.

McCaul, Bill, Dr. "Tornado Myths." Tornado Project Online. December 15, 2012 www.tornadoproject.com.

"Planning for a Stronger Alabama." Tornado Recovery Action Council of Alabama. December 15, 2012 www.tracalabama.org.

Rice, Doyle. "Despite 2011, Study Shows Tornadoes Not Getting Worse." USA Today. 23 October 2012.

Scripture quotations marked NIV are taken from the Holy Bible, New International Version ®Copyright 1973, 1978, 1984 by International Bible Society. All rights reserved.

Smith, Jewell Ellen. Sunbonnet Soliloquy. "Stars Fell on Alabama" (November 18, 1833).

"Super Outbreak." Wikipedia. December 15, 2012 http://en.wikipedia.org/wiki/super_outbreak.

Taylor, Barbara Brown. "Tell Us a Resurrection Story." Getting Read for Sunday. December 15, 2012 www.gettingreadyforsunday.com.

"TOR:CON Index." The Weather Channel. December 15, 2012 www.weather.com/news/tornado/torcon-index.

Walton-Raji, Angela Y." The Night the Stars Fell-My Search for Amanda Young."My Ancestor's Name. Friday, April 2, 2010. December 16, 2012 www.myancestorsname.blogspot.com.

Weather related statistics and measurements were taken from the National Oceanic and Atmospheric Administration (NOAA) website, specifically the National Weather Service, unless otherwise noted. December 15, 2012 www.noaa.gov.

ABOUT THE AUTHOR

Shelly Van Meter Miller was born in Owensboro, KY. She graduated from Murray State University with a Bachelor of Science in Speech Communication. After college, she worked as a press aide for a United States Senator in Washington, D.C. before marrying her husband and settling in Madison, Alabama.

Together, she and her husband raised three girls in the South. While residing in Huntsville for a quarter of a century, Shelly has seen the destruction caused by violent tornadoes that have affected her life and the lives of those around her. She has watched her town rebuild more than once and considers Alabama her home.

She taught aerobics and pregnancy exercise classes throughout the community and even completed a half-marathon. Yes, you read it correctly, "half." She considers that to be good enough. She then homeschooled her children and exercised her writing muscle by grading stacks of research papers. She was fired from that job when her children went to public school.

Nowadays, Shelly finds her muse in the garden. She became a Master Gardener to have an excuse to work at what she loves. Her ideal day is spent writing in the garden. Careful, because if you ask her what she does all day, she will say "nothing," unless she is chasing her three cats.

If you enjoyed this book, I'd appreciate it if you would leave an honest review. I'd love to hear from you and appreciate your comments. I am very interested in hearing your tornado stories. You can get in touch with me at http://www.tornadovalley.net or shelly@tornadovalley.net.

Shelly Van Meter Miller

Made in the USA
Middletown, DE
04 September 2024

60264678R00106